The Future of Love

Also by Daphne Rose Kingma

Coming Apart

A Garland of Love

The Men We Never Knew

Weddings from the Heart

Heart & Soul

Finding True Love

The Future of Love

The Power of the Soul
in Intimate Relationships

Daphne Rose Kingma

MAIN STREET BOOKS

Doubleday
New York London Toronto Sydney Auckland

A MAIN STREET BOOK
PUBLISHED BY DOUBLEDAY
a division of Random House, Inc.
1540 Broadway, New York, New York 10036

MAIN STREET BOOKS, DOUBLEDAY, and the portrayal of a building with a tree are
trademarks of Doubleday, a division of Random House, Inc.

Designed by Brian Mulligan

The Library of Congress has cataloged the Doubleday edition as follows:
Kingma, Daphne Rose.
    The future of love: the power of the soul in intimate relationships / by Daphne Rose
Kingma. — 1st ed.
        p.   cm.
    1. Intimacy (Psychology).   2. Interpersonal relations.   3. Love.   I. Title.
    BF575.I5K55   1998
    158.2′4—dc21   97-32109
                                                                                  CIP

ISBN 0-385-49084-4

First Main Street Books Edition: February 1999

10 9 8 7 6 5 4 3 2 1

For F.X.
with abiding love

Acknowledgments

My deep thanks to those who, in love, delivered me here:
F. X. Feeney, William Edward Glennon, and, most especially,
Mary Jane Ryan.

Very special thanks
To Marianne Williamson for loving encouragement, spiritual
kinship, and sacred witness; and to Al Lowman for
magnificent literary nurturing, and also for generosity and
poetry and dignity. You are a gift, Al.

Special thanks also
To JK007 for extraordinary love and generosity and for going
all the way through this with me.
To Ian McLeod McKnockiter for encouragement from across
the sea and across all worlds.
To William Claude Slater for being, once again, the miracle.
To B. G. Dilworth, Charlotte Patton, Dean Williamson, and
Maggie Lang for always being so graciously there.
To Andrea Cagan for friendship, editorial assistance, and soul
kindness.
To Pat Mulcahy, my editor at Doubleday, for being

courageous, receptive, responsive, and wonderfully real; and to Denell Downum for handling every transaction in the preparation of this book with the utmost graciousness.

Warm thanks

To Laura Madsen, the Angel of Responsibility, for steadfastness, intelligence, and an ever-lovely spirit.

To Kym Rousseau, the Delightful One, for cheering my heart and smoothing my path.

To Donald McIlraith for being an open heart and a healing hearth.

To my dear sister, Chris, for being there every step of the way.

And much love to Molly, who's been there all along.

Contents

Foreword

Sometimes you *can* judge a book by its cover.

A couple of years ago I bought a book by Daphne Rose Kingma for no other reason, I'm afraid to say, than that I liked the title, and the gorgeous jacket matched my bedroom decor. What the heck, I thought—this book begs for a silver teapot, and who knows, I might even read it.

When the day came, not too long after, when I began to do just that, I found one of those delicious treats awaiting me: reading a book that no one has yet told you is amazing, but which certainly is. What followed was the usual celebratory ritual: call all your girlfriends, buy as many of the books as you can for all of them. "This woman," I said, *"totally* understands."

It was one of those books you're so enthralled by that you read every last word on the jacket, and lo and behold, guess what I found? Daphne Rose Kingma, announced the jacket, lives in *my town.* And so I wrote a fan letter, and have been sitting at her feet ever since.

One day, sharing with Daphne a relationship quagmire of my own, I said to her, "I read your book—I thought you could fix me!"

"Not with *that* book," she answered. *"You're* about my *next* book."

And her next book is what you now hold in your hands. As I write this, I don't know yet what its cover looks like, but I know the power of its content and the radical—and radically transforming effect—of its information. I have been listening to Daphne Rose Kingma for over a year now, hanging on to her words because I know they come from somewhere very deep and far away. I think she is one of the Knowers on the planet, one of the women who see things, and pass on the information. With this book, I hope her information reaches even further and wider, past our personalities, past our barriers, past our resistances to love. She takes our hands and guides us past the war zones of relationships to the peaceful meadows of a higher love.

The only thing this book can't give you is the marvel of her face, her hands, her body, her laughter, her mischievous sparkling knowing eyes, and—excuse me for throwing this in—her taste in clothes. But you can still get so much magic from this book. Daphne Rose Kingma is a spiritual power-house who enters your life and does amazing things. With this book, she carries on her work. So settle in, reader. You're in excellent hands.

—Marianne Williamson

A Renaissance of Love

Love is a mighty power. It is light. It is the energy of life. It brings us into life and sustains us while we live and breathe.

Love is an energy, not a substance. It is essence, not matter. You can't contain it; you can't put it in a box, but you can feel it, taste it, and know it. Its presence is unmistakable. It is exquisite and profound. And when you are in love, nobody, not your best friend, your parents, or even your own mind can talk you out of it.

Love is mysterious and beautiful. It makes us happy, gives us hope, allows us to believe that the impossible can happen.

And yet, it's inexplicable. It can't be defined or analyzed, catalogued or priced. Its premier property is that when it exists, it can never be mistaken for anything else, and nothing else, no matter how worthwhile or supposedly grand, can ever be passed off as love.

Love is a divine energy that steps into human circumstances, a timeless essence that enters time. It is older, wiser, finer, truer, sweeter, and more radiant than any human being. It is what makes us wise, fine, true, sweet, and radiant. It is the best—the essence of God—in us. And it is love, this exquisite energy, with which we connect when we first enter into the human experience we call "a relationship." We see this energy in one another's eyes; we feel it in our bodies and we know that something bigger than life has stepped into our lives to capture our attention. It is this highly charged, buoyant, transcendent, delicious feeling, and the longing for more, for a lifetime of it, that propels us into relationships.

Relationships are the endless interplay of this vast energy of love and all that occurs in our daily human lives. Our desire to feel this love forever, to be in love always, to repeat and endlessly recapture this ecstatic luminous feeling day by day, year after year, with the person who first inspired it in us is not only why we "fall in love" but also why we choose "to have relationships." It is also why, when our relationships go sour or grow threadbare, we reminisce about the way they once were. We want to reconnect with love.

Our greatest desire is to have our relationships return us again and again to the transforming and beautiful experience of the love that first inspired them and brought them into being. We live to love.

If all of this is true about love, and I believe it to be, then why are we so often disappointed in the love in our lives? Why does it so often seem to fail us and why is it so often a pitched battle?

Like so many of the rest of us, I am a veteran of the relationship wars, and by profession I am also a diplomat in love's peacekeeping operations. I've entered and ended more than a dozen fully formed intimate relationships, ranging from conventional marriage to passionate interludes that ran their course, then ended. In some I left; in others I was left. In some I was betrayed; in others I was the betrayer. A few ended in anger, many more ended by creating the portal to a new and deeper connection, allowing the love that had infused them to become even more profound after the relationship's so-called demise.

I've written more than half a dozen books about relationships from the point of view that an intimate relationship is the ultimate container of love in the human experience. As I wrote these books about the traditional forms of relationship, urging people toward the enchantments of romance and the fulfillments of marriage, I watched as my own relationships broke the rules of convention and assumed surprising and extraordinary forms. At first I thought this was just me, but then I realized that everyone I was counseling was also living in relationships that were in conflict with their own definitions of what a relationship should be. Their relationships, too, were turning somersaults and taking on forms that shocked them, and the very strangeness of all this change was sowing a sense of confusion and disaster.

In fact, these startling, new relationships, which conventional minds might call aberrant, are actually Roman candles lighting the way to a world of new possibility. Something wonderful is happening in all this chaos, but nobody knows what it is. Everybody in this position is thinking, "Other people have *real* relationships. What's the matter with me?"

There's nothing the matter with any of us, but there is a grand transformation afoot. A mysterious energy seems to be quietly taking over, and things, we may say, just aren't the way they used to be. When we say this, we're not like our grandmothers, crotchety in their rocking chairs, lamenting the passing of the past. A new world, a new way of being, is being born in our midst. We can feel it.

Things are categorically different. Time has a strange new quality. It passes before we have a moment to rest in it. There's a new softness in our midst, a way of being with one another, that is gracious and gentle and kind. There is also a beautiful strangely infiltrating awareness, a mystic pulse of connection that seems to be gathering us together. Love is trying to find us.

And in the process, all the forms are changing. Our whole world of relationships is in an uproar. Love is the wrecking ball that is pulverizing every relationship of record that isn't wide enough or brave enough to let real love in. As a consequence, we can't fantasize anymore about what our relationship lives will be. The truth is that exceptions and aberrations abound. It's as if we awakened one morning to discover that a blizzard of transformation occurred during the night. The new world has its strange beauty. Familiar landmarks are vaguely, heartwarmingly still visible beneath the blanket of snow, but it's treacherous out there. We're cold, we long for the hearth; we want to come home.

This book is about the breaking down of relationships as we have known them, the subsequent emergence of new forms of relatedness, and the future of love. It is about a journey we're already taking. We have been moving backwards, forwards, and sideways into the future, moving away from a place that was dear and familiar and sweet toward a world that is strange and forbidden.

Having been raised to regard marriage as the only honorable relationship, we woke up to discover that it was only one in a vast array of intimate connections. Our relationships are about our hearts, and all this chaos is breaking our hearts. We don't know whether to go along with all this transformation or resist it, whether to think of it as some kind of progress or to dig in our heels, praying for a reprieve from all this harrowing evolution.

The truth is, we have all come from love, but our relationships have often been a detour from love. I believe that we were all together once, as a single, vast, pulsating, luminous consciousness that was divided bit by bit, person by person, into the tiny, shining fragments that are our individual souls. Love is the river, each human being a droplet of water, and together, in spite of our fears and resistance, we are returning to love, melting and flowing toward home.

We're all looking for more love. It's that simple. In the end, nothing else really matters to us. In the beginning and in the middle, we're concerned with the forms of our relationships, what they look like, what our parents think of them, how they stack up in the eyes of the world, and whether we're getting our share of the goodies: sexually, emotionally, and financially.

But in the end, we won't care about the forms. The forms will be as multitudinous as the stars and all that will matter is the love that was in them. No one can escape the divine upheaval of love. I haven't; you won't; your neighbors and strangers and family won't either. Love is coming to find us. All of us. Because love is our essence. Love is who we are.

Chapter 1

Awakening Spiritual Consciousness

Relationships as
the Chalice of Love

We have always had relationships, because in human experience our intimate relationships are the chalice of our love. When we fall in love, it is love that takes us to them, and it is love, we hope, that will abide with us in them.

But relationships as we have known them are over. And love as we live it is being born anew. If you haven't already encountered this truth in your own life, then all you have to do is look around. Our relationship lives are falling apart. There isn't one of us who hasn't had an agony or a heartbreak, a shattering divorce or a frightening night alone on the couch. Life has defied our mythic picture of what a "real relationship" should look like. And although from within our own poignant experience we know that relationships aren't the solution to everything, we still keep seeking them, wanting them, hoping they will make us totally happy, that they will give us ourselves.

That the form is no longer working is everywhere evident. Within the space of a few months recently, I encountered the following people: a woman, supposedly happily married and the mother of a young child, who, to fulfill her emotional needs, is having two outside sexual relationships. A woman, married two times unsuccessfully and finally, a third glowingly romantic and heartfelt time, who is finding herself, after ten years of this third "perfect" marriage, divorcing once again. A divorcée enjoying a platonic relationship with a married man who lives hundreds of miles away who is also carrying on simultaneous sexual relationships with two men in her hometown, and exploring, with a committed, serious group that holds regular monthly meetings, alternative forms of relationships. A middle-aged man, married two times and the father of three young sons who has just sent off his third paramour for a one-year postgraduate sabbatical in Europe with the blessing that "every man who's your lover while I'm gone is a brother of mine." The unmarried mother of a nine-year-old daughter who has had a twenty-five-year-long affair with a married man who is not her daughter's father. An unmarried mother of a young son who has no sexual relationship but an abiding emotional intimacy of ten years' duration with a man she considers to be her "emotional husband." A woman in her mid-forties, never married, who has had a seven-year weekend relationship with a gay man who also has a male lover. A widow with children, married for the second time, who embraced two stepchildren only to be widowed again and find herself the single parent of four fatherless children, two of which were not her own. A man in his forties, never married, whose entire relationship life is conducted with a bevy of beautiful women, some of whom are his lovers, some not, but who, all together, fulfill his emotional and libidinous needs. A man in his early thirties who is having a relationship with a woman in her early fifties and contemplating marrying her. An unmarried woman in her late forties who is considered "single," but has never been without an intimate relationship for more than three weeks.

As extraordinary as all the *forms* of these relationships may be, they certainly demonstrate that, fundamentally, we are relational beings. We don't live in isolation; our entire lives are lived in a matrix of relationships. We are born into relationships and we live out our lives in relationships. Indeed our personalities take on their unique forms and colorations through the multitude of experiences that, as human beings, we have in relationships.

A relationship of any form is a configuration of connection. It is the vessel in which we mix ourselves with others, the container in which, together with them, we hold ourselves in a certain way. Our entire experience of being alive is about relationship. We are related to ourselves, our parents and children, our houses and jobs, to nature, to history, to the planets and all the stars, to the weather and its effects on us, to sound and its effects on us, to the sky, to music, to art, to magic, to our pasts and futures, and to life and death.

When we speak of "a relationship," however, we're usually

modifying or glorifying our general understanding of the concept of relatedness to refer to some very specific ways in which we connect with one another. So it is that we speak of "being in love," having "an intimate relationship," "a sexual relationship," "a romance," or "a marriage." But whatever its name, a relationship is always a way we connect with another human being. It is a connection that shows not only how near or far we've decided to be, but also how dearly or uniquely we hold this person in our hearts, and what we hope will come to pass with them in our lives. It also says something about the potential for how happy or miserable we may become as we occupy this special stance, this unique pattern of connection called "a relationship" that we have undertaken with them.

Relationships Are Ever-Changing

We tend to think of relationships as static, as if we could just get into them, assume a position inside them and then continue to hold it, essentially without changing, forever, world without end. But in fact, our relationships are fluid, vivid, mercurial, and constantly changing.

Your relationship to your infant is different from your relationship to your twelve-year-old daughter, for example; as your relationship to her as an adolescent is different from your relationship to her as a woman of forty with children of her own. You fall in love with the young man who lives around the corner—he's there for a summer vacation—but has a burgeoning career in music that takes him to South Africa. You say goodbye to him for eight months, marry him when he returns, discover he has a contract to work in Los Angeles, pack up your things to join him there, and live with him there for three years. When smog, freeways, and overwork put your relationship at risk, you have a powwow and decide to move to Vermont.

We start out in a relationship in a certain destined moment—instantly falling madly in love, making a touching friendship at school, intoxicating ourselves on vacation with a romantic interlude—but then the calendar rolls, the moment passes, the configuration of our connection revises, and one way or another we move on. We move on within the relationship, or we move on to other relationships. Our relationships are always re-forming, changing, redefining themselves.

As children we leave our houses and families. As lovers we separate by moving across town, going away to college. As married people we split up because of irreconcilable differences, or death, or, over time, we simply and beautifully evolve together, because of the journey that love takes us on.

Work, circumstances, the passage of time all profoundly affect our relationships. So do our emotions. The ebullient blush of first love may diminish like the proverbial bloom on the rose with the passage of time—"you used to be so . . ." or "we used to be so . . ." Or, in a remarkably beautiful variation on what we sometimes imagine to be the unavoidable natural diminution of feelings, many relationships deepen, expand, progress, and flower ever more beautifully as they age.

I know a couple, a university librarian and a professional diver, introduced by mutual friends, who, when they first met, felt they really had nothing in common. Yet because of the vacancies in their lives they continued "to see one another." Their courtship was homely, comprised of the very few things that they could actually comfortably share—an occasional movie, Sunday afternoon walks in the local botanical garden. They both surrendered to these outings as pleasant enough digressions from their demanding and somewhat lonely lives. But as time went on and their afternoon jaunts continued, they gradually opened themselves to deeper levels of conversation. They discovered they shared many values—a commitment to the environment, to sharing their financial resources with the less fortunate, a quiet but deeply spiritual view of life, a conviction about personal integrity.

Gradually, they found themselves becoming acquainted; surprisingly, they found themselves falling in love. Remarkably, they were wonderful lovers. Astonishingly, they got married. Beautifully, over time, their respect and their love have expanded. Of their relationship journey they say, "We're the most unlikely, most mismatched couple we know. Our friends had the courage to bring us together; but it was our willingness to let the relationship unfold week by week, circumstance by circumstance, that has taken us to where we are."

No matter how "stable, steady, static, or settled" we hope our relationships will be, the passage of time, things that come in from left field, out of the blue, or off the wall—the six million dollars you inherit from the aunt you thought was only moderately wealthy, the cancer that gets diagnosed two weeks after your honeymoon, the child you inherit when your spouse's ex-wife decides to go on an African safari—all somersault our relationships into the actual powerful journeys they are. Life goes through us as we go through it, and our relationships are affected as a consequence.

Far from being rigid, relationships are a miraculous, organic process. Just as each time we take a new breath we both inhale and exhale, there is also an organic rhythm to our intimate connections. There is a rhythmic movement to our breathing, a coming and going, an entering and departing. Between these actions is an exquisite moment of stillness in which the essence of life occurs. Like breathing, like the tides and seasons change, so, too, do our relationships. Just as we breathe both in and out, there is an incoming and outgoing energy in all our intimate connections. The very essence of any relationship is movement.

Relationships Are Self-Creating

But relationships aren't just an ever-changing process of movement; they are also a journey of self-creation. That is, we are always creating and re-creating ourselves through them. We discover who we are, become more of ourselves, get better or worse, fatter or thinner, more spiritually conscious or more thuddingly unaware through them. It is through our connections with others that we continue to meet ourselves and, over time, develop to our fullest.

"I'm a sister," you might say, "because in my family I'm one of five children," or "I'm a lover, because I make love with my beloved." Or "I'm a mother, because I gave birth to a child." All these ways of describing ourselves have to do with specific positions we hold and even roles we occupy with one another, and as much as they define us, what is even more mysterious and beautiful is that we become different, more or less of what we are, precisely because of these relational connections. So it is that you may not only discover your intelligence through your closeness to a dear intelligent friend, but you will also *become* more intelligent because of your association with her. That's because this proximity in itself—this relationship—allows something of her to "rub off" on you. So it is that we are not only able to identify our selves through our relational proximities—sister, lover, mother, friend—but we are actually transformed by them.

Relationships keep changing us because as personalities and as spirits we are always growing. That is our human quest; it's what we're here for. And our relationships shift, shape, change, and re-form us not only as time passes, but also as the people who move through them with us go through changes of their own.

When I was a college freshman, I was strangely intrigued by the classic beginning philosophy student's question: If the tree falls in the forest, but nobody sees it falling, has the tree actually fallen?

At the time, this concept was just an intellectual mind-tangle, but it pointed at something we are all now discovering—that everything affects and exists in relationship to everything else. Physicists tell us that the world of energy and matter is a relational world, that every particle exists and can be identified as itself only through its relationship to other particles. We know New York because of its dissimilarity to and distance from Paris; Columbus because of its distance from Decatur.

It's the same way with each of us and our relationships. We

not only see who we are through them—*Jane is different from Dick, her husband*. But we also *become* more of who we are precisely because of them—*Jane is prettier now that she's married to Dick*. Perhaps because Dick sees her, Jane becomes more beautiful; perhaps because someone is there to witness it, the tree gladly falls in the forest. We are able to see who we are because of who we stand beside; we become who we are because of who loves us. We become more beautiful or strong, more tender or magnificent. Relationships change us and shape us.

Relationships Are Everywhere

Many of us tend to think of "a relationship" as the unique pairing that we have always called marriage, but we are constantly, endlessly, being shaped by many different kinds of relational encounters. You are related to the man on the side street who swerves his car, and thereby misses you by inches, the waitress who brings you your glass of wine, and the doctor who administers your anesthesia. All these encounters may be only the minutest instances of relationship; nevertheless, they affect you and you are changed and shaped by them.

Like me, you've probably had the experience of walking down a street, and noticing a beautiful woman some distance off who's walking in your direction. She may still be far away, and yet it seems that the very focus of your attention is drawing her importantly toward you. And perhaps a few minutes later, as you pass one another on the sidewalk, without skipping a step, you acknowledge one another with a smile. At that moment, you've stopped being an observer; you have entered into relationship. This woman, who only moments ago was a stranger, has responded to the expression of your energy. However minutely, she has entered your world and affected you, too. You have both been affected. Whatever the ultimate consequence of the encounter—as small as a smile, as immense as a love affair—you have entered into a relationship.

In fact, this is what a relationship is: it is the way we affect one another through the power of our proximity and the energy of our consciousness. What this means is that we're not just standing still, holding a specific static position in relation to another person, nor are we just witnessing the changing position of that other person, tree, or object. We are actually *affecting* that person, creature, or thing through the power of our proximity—just as their proximity is in some way affecting us. In each relational encounter we are bringing all of who we are, and every person with whom we step into relationship, even momentarily, is feeling and responding to our energy and consciousness, the whole of who we are. Other people are developing, changing, becoming more of themselves through you, and you are becoming more of yourself through them. In this way, your personality is acting on other people in a vibrant relational matrix all the time. Indeed, we have no neutral moments. We are all always related; we are always affecting one another. We are all always *in relationship*. And this experience of relationship isn't incidental or puny; it is life-changing and profound.

Our Intimate Relationships

Our intimate relationships are a much more intense and specific version of this experience of relational connection. Until now, we've always looked at what we've generally agreed to call "a relationship" from a particular understanding of what we all meant by an intimate relationship. This has usually meant partnerships between two people, usually a man and a woman (more recently sometimes two men or two women), which had certain homely and comely attributes that brought us the sense that we could truly find comfort in them. Our "relationships," as we fondly called them, were daily affairs based on a sexual connection; they had roofs and houses and walls. They were exclusive; we found a single person to love and remain faithful to. They were for always; we promised to love one another forever.

But now it's these same relationships that aren't working. They end; they don't look or behave the way they used to, the way we thought they should. They're breaking our hearts and falling apart at the seams. Half of our marriages end in divorce, and who knows how many of our trial, practice, and part-time loves are also crashing on the rocks. By now none of us has passed through the tunnel of love unscathed, and as the century plows to an end, we are both dying and coming of age as lovers.

Awakening Spiritual Consciousness

We are living in a totally gorgeous and challenging time in history in which a spiritual consciousness is arising in our midst. In Western culture, this means that we are moving from the awareness that we are personalities to the recognition that we are spiritual beings. We are gradually becoming aware of the fact that we are not just people leading lives composed of all the events and components we ordinarily think of as being our "real" lives, but eternal spirits who have entered human history. This awareness is approaching us on every hand. Although we have lived through a technologically brilliant century, fascinated with our own achievements, our capacity to earn and spend, to conquer and invent, to create machines that defy the gods and unify—or terrify—our fellow man, we have come to the place where all these undertakings no longer entirely satisfy us.

The same is true of our relationships. We have wanted them to give us everything, to be the be-all and end-all of our existence, to solve all our problems, to make life worth living, to give us ourselves, but they haven't quite been able to do this. Interestingly, the reason we have elevated relationships to this godlike level is that we think of ourselves only as personalities, the sum total of all our attributes and experiences within a given lifetime. As personalities, we have wanted to experience love. Love satisfies us. We know ourselves best when we love, and so as personalities we have expected our relationships—and usually a *single* relationship—to be a total experience of love.

We emphasize the personality because we live in a psychological culture. This means that we are focused on the individual person—his well-being, history, wants, needs, and fulfillments. For this entire century, since Freud discovered the id, the ego, and the unconscious we have been studying and perfecting our psychological selves. We are blessed and lucky to have learned as much as we have about our personalities, to know that we have unconscious as well as conscious experience, that there are hidden as well as obvious motives that direct us. We have delighted and enthralled ourselves with the exploration of these mysterious layers of ourselves, and in our culture that exploration has been equivalent to a religious undertaking.

But just as this century has seen the unfolding of the beautiful complexities of our personalities, we are now at the brink of another level of awakening. New possibilities of harmony and illumination are all around us, attending us as we stand at the threshold of full awareness of who we really are: human spiritual beings.

It's not that this is news exactly; hardly a soul among us has passed through this life without having a moment of spiritual awakening—music so ecstatic that it brings tears to your eyes; encountering someone you haven't seen for decades on a street corner in a city you've never been to before; staring up at the clouds and becoming suddenly one with them as you lie on the grass; hearing a voice that, from nowhere, speaks a truth you needed to hear. All these are actions of spirit in our midst. We now also speak of angels; we now talk about our souls.

Even our emotions—that ever-flowing river of our feelings—are trying to tell us that the consciousness that lies within our bodies, that what we experience as anger and delight, sorrow and self-pity, is far more than just another psychological layer. It is an energy embodied, a whoosh of divine consciousness within our mortal selves that is trying to awaken us to the fact that we are not just bodies and minds, but souls who have taken on bodies in the human evolutionary adventure we call life.

Our world has started to change and we are changing with it. Given all this change, when it comes to our relationships, we've gone about as far as we can go; we've gotten as much as we can reasonably expect on the personality level. We have drowned ourselves in self-help books, marriage encounter workshops, communication seminars—not that these things aren't all of value—but our relationships still aren't perfect. And we're starting to understand that maybe they never will be. We've approached them from the point of view that they're perfectible, that they can give us ultimate satisfaction. But they can't. They haven't yet and they never will, because our personalities are not entirely who we are.

What is happening now in the world of our relationships is that our wholeness is emerging. Our personalities are longing to come of age. They're sick of the struggle. They want something better, more beautiful, easier. Just as a child finally gets tired of crawling on hands and knees, so our personalities are longing to come into the larger awareness that we are spiritual beings whose one true vocation is love.

We have come to this now not just because we're bored with crawling but because, as with the child who finally delights in learning to walk, this is a natural progression. We want to mature our love, to be able to love more—more people, more ways, more easily, and with more joy. And we want to do this also because there is a force both inside and outside of us that is now not only suggesting but insisting that we come into the maturity of this full awareness of ourselves.

Every age has had its threshold of awakening, and this is ours. Just as the human understanding of the world moved from thinking it was flat to knowing it was round, just as our awareness shifted from the belief that ours was a single galaxy to the astonishing knowledge that it is only one of billions, so this force—Love, God, the Soul, whatever you choose to call it—is striking our hearts to an awakening of our true magnificence as human spiritual beings.

Why is this happening now? you may ask. Because it's time. And we're ready. God, that force, that Love, that profoundly beautiful energy that gave us life and holds us gently in its cradle, has invited us into the awareness that until now, has been only the tinkling of an enchanted bell of remembrance. It chimes each time we fall in love, each time we are magnificent in one of our relationships, each time we trust or surrender or forgive, each moment we live in the truth, each time we blossom with compassion. All this beauty is now being asked to come into our relationships.

It's very simple. God wants us to wake up now. God wants us to know each other as spirits as well as personalities, to embrace our lives as the exquisite spiritual journeys they are, and to deliver us from the tedious, frustrating, and ultimately unsatisfying ordeals that our relationships become when we live them only at the personality level.

When I was a little girl, I was taken to the Natural History

Museum and there I watched while, under warm glowing lightbulbs, a dozen adorable baby chicks pecked their way out of their eggs. I'd always thought it would be easy, that just the thought of coming out into a world so full of clear light and green trees and grass would be enough to entice a chicken out of its egg, but it was a shockingly laborious undertaking. That day I also learned that chickens only come out of their shells because they are literally dying to be born. By the time they start this exhausting pecking process, the insides of their shells are so contaminated that if they didn't blast their way out, they would be suffocated by the very environments that once protected them.

We, too, are dying to be born. It is time now for us to unleash ourselves from the psychological swaddling clothes of this past century, to clatter our way into the bright world of our spiritual consciousness. We have no choice. Our souls are insisting upon it because the quality of love with which we have created our relationships is no longer large enough, rich enough, or beautifully illumined enough to nurture us in our true dimension, which is spiritual.

Our souls want us to be born in full consciousness in this life, on this earth, at this time. What our personalities have learned, the maturity we have developed, and even all the healing we have accomplished for them is no longer enough for our souls.

This transformation will take effort; at times it will even be painful. But what we need to remember is that we are being given an opportunity to come to our spiritual awareness *through our relationships,* where we already seek and speak of love. The sweet thing is that we are being invited to come to this awakening in a form which is so familiar to us that it is one of the greatest traditions of all of human history. We have always fallen in love; love is what has always awakened our hearts and allowed us not only to imagine but to actually feel in the threads of our veins that there is something larger, more profound, and more exquisite than anything we ourselves have created or can undertake.

This is the moment. We are being invited to move from falling in love to loving, from romance to true love, from relationships that are an undertaking of the personality to unions that are illumined by the soul. We are being asked to mature into our true wholeness, as human beings who are in fact divine eternal souls, and we are being invited to do this *in relationship*.

A journey we started as personalities we are now being asked to finish as souls. This will mean many things. First, giving up the idea that "a relationship" will be perfect; second, most likely, having more than one significant relationship in a lifetime; third, breaking out of the forms as we have known them; fourth, loving more, in different ways, with perhaps a less personal and certainly a less self-involved focus; and fifth, operating from spiritual principles day to day in our relationships.

We will be able to do all this only if we can understand how dearly and badly our personalities have needed love in the past, and how urgently our souls need love now. As with the chicken cracking the egg, the containers are breaking open so we can move into freedom. Some of the journey will be arduous. At times it won't seem fair. But we don't have any choice. And there will be angels along the way.

The future of love is true love, a great, sweet love that isn't pain but joy, not small, but vast, not personal but spiritual. This is where we are going; this is our true destination. But before we can arrive there, we must look first at the journey we've already taken. What was it? Why did we need to take it? What has it given to us? And how, now that our time has come, may we graciously move on?

By looking at where we've been, what we've been up to, so to speak, in our relationships, we can begin to discern where we need to go and what the beautiful future will look like when we arrive.

Chapter 2

The Past as Prologue

Relationships as Social Convention

Ours is a marrying culture, and since marriage is our traditional picture of a relationship, if we want to be loved in this culture, sooner or later we have to get married. We don't say this, of course, and we have many actual relationships that are not marriage, but in our hearts we hanker after marriage, and in our society "marriage" is the relationship norm. Given the power of marriage in our culture, if you want to be loved, you have four options:

1. You can be married.
2. You can be waiting to be married.

3. You can be a person who has suffered divorce and is subsequently waiting to marry again.
4. Or, God forbid, you can be a person who is single and was never blessed with an opportunity to marry in the first place.

It isn't socially acceptable *not* to want to "get married" or *not* to "be in a relationship." That's because the longing for marriage is so entrenched in our collective unconscious that it is one of our most powerful personal motivations. It's the way we both inspire ourselves and beat ourselves up. We inspire ourselves because the thought of marriage brings us joy, and we beat ourselves up because so often we "fail" at marriage: we never find a suitable marriage partner; if we find one, we can't seem to make our marriages stick; or by being gay we are perpetually standing outside the walls of conventional marriage.

All our intimate relationships are measured by the marriage model. We see it as the union we desire; *the* sacred union for lovers; our relationship of record, and the form of relationship that will give us the most comfort and offer us the most love. That's why even after communes, free love, and women's liberation, marriage is seeing a huge resurgence. And that is also why people excluded from it—gay people who want to marry, for example—want to partake of it, and why many heterosexual people feel threatened by the thought of its being encroached upon.

Why is the archetype of marriage so potent? Because it's so ancient, because it's been with us for centuries. In fact, marriage has been around for so long that most of us don't even know where it came from. Ethnologists tell us that the earliest forms of marriage were a sort of communal gathering together for the purpose of ensuring the survival of the species. People cleaved to one another, not because they "fell in love" or because they could discover or fulfill themselves in "a relationship," but because their joining assured procreation and protection for the young, and thus secured the survival of the species.

How we have lived our intimate lives over the past two millennia at least and how we think of relationships now in our hearts are the long inheritance of this primal need for survival and of our social need to be gathered and protected. It is out of these very basic human concerns that the beliefs we hold about our intimate relationships developed.

What began as a tribal gathering in which specific partners were often chosen by the head of the tribe or the parents of those who would marry, was later made sacred as marriage in Christian culture and, through the rise of the concept of romantic love, became that passionate joining of a man and woman that we have come to cherish as marriage. Over time, the concept of marriage has been woven more and more deeply into the social fabric in such a way that it both encourages the creation of such relationships and supports them in their being. (A simple example of this is that the U.S. government supports marriage by giving tax incentives to those who are legally married and not to individuals or to individuals merely living together.)

As the centuries passed, laid over the issue of survival was the notion of romantic love, the idea that love was a matter of sexual attraction and a swooning of the heart. Deep feelings of passionate attachment were considered appropriate between individuals, in fact they became the raison d'être of "a relationship." Eventually, marriage, which had originally been created purely for survival reasons, began to be the container in which all such romantic feelings were also to be enacted. Love, a matter of the heart, became enfolded with social convention.

Now, although relationships have evolved far beyond the need for protection and survival—childbearing women of the 1990s don't need the same kind of protection that cave women once did, and we certainly don't need any more people on the face of the earth—these deep memories of our need for survival and our desire for romance still reside within us. So no matter how far our relationships have actually progressed, no matter that millennia have passed, or even that we've spent the last century exploring our psychological selves and are now emerging as spiritual beings, deep down inside we're all still operating by beliefs about our relationships that were coined when our survival depended upon them.

Marriage and Society

The stability of marriage—the idea of two people cleaving together for life—has been so important for our collective survival that our beliefs about marriage became one of the cornerstones of society. Indeed, keeping our relationships on an even keel, having our marriages function as steady, reliable units, whirring cogs in the spinning machinery of our little communities, is what makes "society" what it is, and society is what encourages marriage to be what *it* is.

In order to create social stability, there's an unspoken demand, a sort of atmosphere or fragrance in the air that tells married people to stay married, to behave themselves, to care about the larger things society has to offer, and not to do anything too disruptive, like choosing to live in a commune, running off with the next-door neighbor, or deciding not to pay taxes.

But because this unspoken demand is a function of our social rather than our personal consciousness, it compels married people to abide by external values, to participate in a generic rather than an individual or visionary consciousness. Instead of diving to the internal depths where we might find the wisdom of our hearts (and perhaps come up with startling social solutions or unusual relationship forms—a part-time transcontinental relationship or a once-a-week monogamous commitment, for example), we become like sheep who waddle along with the Joneses. The truth is that marriage—as a relationship—has been appropriated by society, and as it serves society, it often suffocates the individual vivid soul.

Duty, responsibility, and social convention, as important as they are, often take us away from our deepest natural connection with one another—our heartfelt connection—and so, while trying to serve the whole, we can betray or abandon ourselves. Instead of searching our hearts, minds, and consciences for the appropriate forms of our relationships, we let our marriages become watered-down versions of the values of society, instead of vibrant emotional unions that nourish the people within them.

Our social beliefs about marriage are still very deeply ingrained, but as all the changes we're going through are showing, they're starting to lose their power. And, indeed, for us to develop further as personalities and souls, they *must* lose their power. But notions inbred in our collective memory die hard and every person alive today still holds within his or her heart the idea that all our relationships should be lived in a form that resembles marriage.

How It Got to Be This Way

Until at least the twentieth century, we needed our social beliefs about marriage in order to survive. They were the inner recognition of the circumstances required for the human family to get where it was going. Your great-grandparents didn't ask themselves whether they were going to live in romantic bliss, sexual ecstasy, or spiritual enlightenment in their relationships. They took a fancy to one another, followed it up with marriage, and then proceeded to the prairie, the Black Forest, the back forty, the barn, or the battlefield, to do whatever needed to be done. It's because they *did* secure our survival that we were able to emerge at the turn of the twentieth century into the psychological beings we have become. But now we have a new evolutionary assignment, and in order to carry it out, we must see that these notions are no longer relevant.

The Social Myths of an Intimate Relationship

The notions we have about marriage are myths. A myth is a story or an idea that is gradually laid down within the consciousness of a people. It's a tale we invent, a belief we hold, about the way things are—or how they ought to be. For example, the tale of Hansel and Gretel is a myth about the triumph of good over evil, the story of David and Goliath an illumination about purity over power. We have myths—stories we tell ourselves—about society, our parents, and the future. We use them to ground us, to explain reality, our practices, our beliefs, and social institutions.

We also have myths about our intimate relationships—all of them based on the marriage model. They tell us that our relationships should be:

1. Daily—seven days a weeks,
2. Domestic—lived under a shared roof in a house with a yard and a white picket fence,
3. Exclusive—the person we love will be our one and only, and
4. Forever—last until the end of time.

Because of their long history in the human consciousness, we're not especially aware of these myths. They're just there, a yeast in the culture. We hold them very dear, and so we're always trying to create the perfect relationships that will live up to them. In turn, by continually trying to create such relationships, we reinforce the myths within the culture and in our hearts and minds.

As a consequence, they remain a deep truth for us, an essential part of the landscape of our thinking about love. Like the pink-streaked twilight or green trees, they simply abide with us as they have always done. Although they may seem subtle, and therefore inconsequential, they are so powerful that, to some extent, for all of us, they are running the relationship show. They are what we seek to embody when we fall in love; they are what we judge ourselves by when we create—or fail at—our relationships.

No matter what kind of relationship life we create, whether it's a country club marriage, a summer romance, a decades-long living-together adventure, a gay marriage, or a life of sequential marriage-like relationships, we're always dragging along the expectations embodied in these myths. And so, if our relationships aren't daily, aren't lived in a shared household, aren't the embodiment of perfection with one single person, or don't last forever, all we can do is feel as if we've failed.

1. Seven Days a Week

When two people fall in love, there's the expectation that their time together will eventually turn into a daily relationship. We don't fall in love and say, "Now that I love you, it would be nice to see you once every six months, once every six days, or even a couple of times a week."

You may have a haphazard, random schedule when you're courting and testing out the relationship waters. But your unconscious expectation is that at some point your romantic affiliation will be translated into a daily relationship (or if you don't want it to be, that's proof that this is the wrong person for you). You'll wake up together every day, you'll sleep in the same bed every night, you'll share the news of your day and go through the "how was your day?" routine with each other, every day of the week, all the years of your lives. The real goal of intimacy, says this myth, is that instead of "being apart," you'll "be together," and the clear implication is that you will, in fact, be together *every* day. This dailiness is such a basic expectation of any intimate relationship that any deviation from it is considered to be just that—a deviation.

This is the survival myth at its most basic. In the days when marriage was built on the pure and brute necessities of daily life, when men harrowed the fields, and women baked the bread, and together they had to see to it that the covered wagon would make it across the plains, it wasn't possible to conceive of a life of daily separation. For millennia, the actual survival of the species depended upon the power of a man and a woman together to be the united force of assault or resistance against whatever outside elements—lions and tigers and locusts—threatened.

Our cells know that to be together in daily proximity is to survive, and it is this memory that's so difficult to launder out of our consciousness. We haven't yet caught up with the fact that loving someone now doesn't really require that we do it on a daily basis, huddled in the same cave or castle, waking up in the same hay mow or high-rise every single morning.

The downside of daily is that we become too familiar, take one another for granted, weary of seeing one another in our old bathrobes, slippers, and underwear every day. Dailiness in itself can be a drag on the radiance of love. What we imagine will be enhanced by all this togetherness is often just diluted. Within the wonderful accessibility of daily life, we can forget to be grand and gorgeous to one another and instead become

boring and banal. We don't love more, better, or more beautifully; love becomes a habit instead of an exaltation of the
heart.

2. The White Picket Fence

We have also created the myth that our intimate relationships will be domestic, that they'll be lived under a shared
roof, in a household with a shared bathroom, wrinkled tooth-
paste tube, half-empty box of cereal, and the same garage full
of old paint cans and faded Monopoly games. This too creates
great expectations and wreaks havoc in our relationships.

When we fall in love, we expect to create a daily life in a
household with all the chores, cozy undertakings, and plumb-
ing complications that domestic life inevitably contains. This,
too, is a hangover from times when it was necessary to huddle
under the same roof in order not to freeze to death, when we
had to share the material substances of life because they were
so scarce or difficult to come by. This isn't the case anymore.
We don't *have* to hole up together anymore just because of the
scarcity of venison. Even though the necessity has passed,
the habit of our relationships remains. We still nest—and
wouldn't consider doing otherwise—with the person we love.

This nesting habit is a tie not only of property but also of
emotion and of consciousness. We make a connection between
domestic life and magic; we expect to have our most powerful
emotional experiences with the person with whom we "settle
down." In fact, we unconsciously believe that settling down,
in itself, will *create* the powerful emotional experiences. We
have somehow conferred upon the habit of domesticity the
false power to raise our relationships to the highest level of

their embodiment, as if putting ourselves together under one roof will, in and of itself, make love grow.

Unfortunately, this premise doesn't turn out to be true. Or in some cases it turns out to be true in ways we never imagined. "Domestic bliss" all too often becomes domestic boredom, domestic servitude, or domestic violence. So domesticity, the cozy settling into a house with someone, a myth that we think of so fondly, in fact often curtails, instead of enhances, our capacity to experience love. Instead of loving one another, we argue about who's going to do the dishes, or pick up the dry cleaning; we get stranded on the material level and lose sight of the deeper ways we are connected.

Domestic life also brings up our difficult and heated emotional issues. That is because domestic life in itself—life under a shared roof with a person or people whom we supposedly love—reminds us of when we were children in houses with parents and siblings. These were relationships that often hurt, and when we reenter the environment in which we were once wounded, all our emotional issues are either consciously or unconsciously stimulated.

That's why 95 percent of the people who build houses together split up. It's also why many people who have been dating and then start living together break up shortly after they move in. Houses—domestic situations in themselves—have a huge capacity to bring up buried emotions, and when these feelings come up, they're often more than a couple is prepared to handle.

3. *The Be-All and End-All*

The third myth that informs our intimate relationships is that they will be exclusive. And not just sexually exclusive. For although we usually designate our paramount relationship to be defined by a bond of sexual fidelity, the myth of exclusivity has many tentacles. As we generally live it out, it has come to mean exclusivity of many kinds. When we fall in love, we're not just saying, "My, what a wonderful mind you have, it'll be a joy to talk with you over the next fifty years." What we're actually saying is "My, what a wonderful mind you have; I'm also expecting you to be a great lover, a great father, a wonderful Friday night date, my comforter in times of sorrow, my social sidekick, my political compatriot, the person my parents will dote on, as well as my guru, my emotional crying towel, and my First Personal National Bank."

Since a single relationship is expected to perfectly fulfill all our needs in this extravagant and unrealistic way, we naturally tend to exclude all others who might participate in the fulfillment of our needs. While this relieves potential others of possible burdens, and in some ways makes life seem less complicated, it overloads marital partners, who are mere mortals who love you, but not gods who can make your every dream come true. In holding to this myth, we become ridiculously demanding. Any person who loves you will be grand in some areas, hopeless in others, but you'll still expect him—or her—to be your everything. No wonder our relationships often disappoint us. Who could possibly live up to these insane expectations?

4. *Till the End of Our Days*

Hardly anybody I know who got married can still fit into their wedding dress, and yet we expect our marriages to stay the same shape and size in which they started—forever. We also expect this form—marriage—in and of *itself*, to confer certain properties, such as kindness, passion, and housekeeping proclivities, on the individuals within it. The traditional form of marriage implies a sort of unchangingness and a permanent commitment. The expectation is that, once having taken on its particular form, a relationship will continue to occupy it for a lifetime. Not only that, but it will abide in this particular form without taking any detours or interesting off-ramps, without turning any somersaults. A marriage will be true to its form and changeless. Above all, it will endure.

Never mind the cynics who tell us that one out of two marriages currently ends in divorce. Our psyches believe that we've fallen in love forever. We're not getting married saying, "I'll love you as long as it feels good," or "It'll be grand for as long as it lasts." We truly believe that, like lovebirds, we are mated for life. We keep making the vows "until death do us part"—or in New Age parlance "until our spirits take a different path."

In the past, forever wasn't a very long time. When the life span was basically half or less of what it is now (a thousand years ago, the median life span was seventeen), when women died in childbirth, men disappeared at sea, at war, or in the woods with the bears, when anyone could die of the plague, influenza, or TB—forever could be just the twinkling of an eye in a thirty-year life span. Those who survived did have serial relationships, husbands or wives to replace the ones who had died. When these people said "until death do us part," they weren't making a fifty- or sixty-year commitment.

The forever myth can have devastating emotional impact. That's because, of all the myths, it creates the most unrealistic expectations. When a relationship we've entered in good faith—one we have watered and nourished at taproot depth—falls apart in our midst, the myth of forever has failed us, and worse yet, *we* have failed it. Since the myth is our embedded standard, if we're not able to actualize it, there must be something wrong with us. It doesn't seem to matter that so many of our friends have also "failed" at marriage and become part of the divorce statistics. It doesn't matter what we ourselves are actually going through, how miserable we are or how many relationships—even actual marriages—we ourselves may have ended. Hope still springs eternal in the human breast and the myth of a love that lasts forever dies hard. In spite of the millions of exceptions, we want to hang on.

The real problem with this myth is that it defies and denies reality. It's not that somewhere in a given lifetime, you won't have a person to love you until the end. But it most likely will take more than one relationship and perhaps even several marriages (particularly as we live longer and longer) to get you to the one person who will be there on the scene when you breathe your last breath. We don't like to think about it; it's upsetting, but it's true. We will have loves and even marriages that do not last forever.

The Larger Comfort of Marriage

We don't talk about it, and on a conscious level we don't believe it, but at the deepest level, we believe that marriage will protect us from death. Underlying the vows "until death do us part" is the unconscious expectation that death will not part us, that we will not die. Love—and life—will somehow go on, and marriage will be the beach umbrella that protects us from the burning rays of our mortality. We think that love is magic (which it is), that it is larger than life (which it is), and longer than time (which it also, in fact, is). But these truths are only true of the soul, on a spiritual level, and when we apply them within the personality's finite frame they are inappropriate and unrealistic. That's why, for example, we're always more overwhelmed by the death of a young person in a marriage than we are when one of an older couple dies. We expect old people to die, of course, and we're shocked when the young depart, but we are even more wounded and shocked when the young and in love are parted by death.

I knew an exquisite young couple, both with the sweetest of natures, generous and kind, and perfectly mated, whose marriage plummeted to an end when the young bride was killed in a plane crash. At the time they'd been married only three years and had just put a deposit on their first home. The wife, twenty-six and a stewardess, was planning to retire within months so that they could start a family, and it was on one of her last scheduled flights that her plane crashed and she was killed.

Along with finding her young death unthinkable, the question that kept being asked was: but how could this happen to *them? They* were so happily married. The implication was clearly that marriage, the magical form of their love in itself, should have prevented her death.

We don't want to die, and as long as we are in the flowing stream of life, death is unthinkable, irrelevant, and weird. This is as it should be. We shouldn't spend our whole lives moping around, worrying about our mortality. Yet death is unfathomably real, the timeless, mysterious counterpoint to life. It is what makes life vivid, and causes us to know that we are more than mere mortals, endlessly enacting the familiar dramas of our lives. Above all, death is the end of life—life's period and question mark. As such, we fear it, we don't like it, and as much as possible, we'd like to put it out of our minds.

Love, and more specifically, marriage, is what we use to forget about death. As a consequence, the most extravagantly unrealistic expectation we make upon our intimate relationships is that somehow they will not only deliver us from our fear of death but in fact deliver us from death itself.

We don't even realize that we have a fear of death, but we all do. We fear the pain of dying, we fear *not being*, which we can't even imagine. Even deeper down, we fear having wasted our lives. Death is life's big mystery, and we'd like to keep it mysterious. We'd rather not stare down the gun barrel at it. Given all this, we'd like to be distracted from it, and who better to keep our mind off our misery than the person who has plighted us their troth?

A Long and Happy Life

While these myths represent our inner guidance and our social motivation as we set about creating our relationships, they also create very specific emotional expectations as we actually live them out. One of their direct consequences is the expectation that marriage will deliver us to a long and happy life. Although we don't know what this means exactly—in our minds, it's vague and unformed—we do know that we want it. We know—or at least we hope, imagine, dream, and actually expect—that once having fallen in love, everything from now on will be perfect. Our problems will melt away; we won't have fights and irresolvable conflicts; hidden issues won't raise their hairy heads to haunt us, and day after day, we'll simply be happy. That is why, for example, when Charles and Diana had a fairy-tale wedding, we fully expected them to live happily ever after. It is also why, whenever sudden or unexpected rifts appear in our relationships, we are shocked, surprised, or in denial, and find ourselves often unequipped to handle them.

What "a long and happy life" actually means in Western culture, however, is having a lot of things: toys, status, machines, vacations to take, money to leave to your children. It doesn't usually mean committing yourself to the ongoing experience of developing your mutual consciousness, or to the inevitable process of transformation that every relationship exacts.

That's because the American "happy life" is a life of a lot of stuff—houses, cars, clothes, trips, CD players, and TV sets;

phones, computers, blowers, mowers, and washing machines—as much as you can get your hands on. The American vision of marriage is the vision of consumer bliss. The encouragement we have for this is the seduction that sadly claws at us from every corner, from every web site, TV, and billboard, in which we are told every which way that we will be able to indulge ourselves completely and therein we will find happiness.

But all the things we seek to possess are literally, and only, things—objects, credit-card bills, possessions. These things don't reach into and touch the velvet linings of our souls. They keep us hooked on the material world, enticing us to believe that it is really the stuff we can amass, and not the love we feel or the level of consciousness we can attain, that is really of the utmost importance.

Even though many of us have awakened to our psychological selves, to the fact that we are not merely collecting, amassing, consumeroid beings, most of us have yet to realize that we are deeply and always also spiritual beings. In spite of the progress we've made, we're still not operating from the realization that our feelings, our passions, run much deeper than our credit cards. We have yet to realize that our emotions exist on a continuum with spirit, and that the life of the spirit is the one true locus of the long and happy life.

The Tragic Distraction

As we look at all the hidden but immensely powerful expectations that permeate our culture and, as a consequence, all the demands that we are making on our intimate relationships, we see that it's no wonder that they're breaking down and falling apart. Like the camel who, overloaded with one or a dozen too many suitcases, satchels, packages, and trunks, finally crumbles to its knees, our marriages can simply no longer bear up under the load. We've asked everything of marriage, all the things it can actually give us—shelter, company on the path, caring, change, and growth—and all the things that it can't possibly provide—ironclad stability, perfect bliss, the fulfillment of all our emotional needs, deliverance from our fear of death. We've gone wild with our expectations, we've been outrageous with our extravagant hopes, and we've poured all our dreams into a sacred, venerable institution that's been doing its best, but can now no longer possibly contain the magnitude of love that is being urged upon us.

The truth is that we get married in order to have an experience of love, but almost immediately we become distracted from that focus. That's because, although it is our souls that bring us to the moment of falling in love, and it is our souls we recognize in one another's eyes, once we actually start to live out our relationships in real life, the social conventions take over and our relationships dwindle into a social undertaking. The soul recedes; social convention and our personalities take over.

In this smaller frame, marriage and all our intimate relationships become an enactment of some of the lowest common denominators of their actual potential. They become a way to pass the time of life, a traditional undertaking that pleases and distracts us. We can be captivated—and even temporarily satisfied—by the familiar form and sweet conventions of marriage. But we must remember that it is Love, the profound

and beautiful and abiding energy, that underlies all the long-
ings and expectations that we bring to our relationships. And
our souls, the divinely immortal part of ourselves, want more.
The soul wants depth, truth, and union, and the call of the
soul, through all the new forms of relationships that are burst-
ing us out of the britches of tradition, is a call to a much
greater love.

Chapter 3

Love as We Have Known It

Relationships
as an Enterprise
of Personality

As we have seen, our beliefs about all our intimate relationships have their deep roots in the traditions of marriage, and marriage has its deep roots in our primal need for survival. In the past century, however, we have been somewhat lifted away from these deeply ingrained conventions and into the world of our psyches. We have been moving from a social to a psychological focus, from a pursuit of survival to the awakening of emotional awareness, from attention to our outer circumstances to a fascination with our inner selves.

Our relationships have joined in this movement, becoming less of a social and more of a personal undertaking. Indeed, it has been the pleasure and pastime of virtually this entire century to become entranced with our emotional lives, and to use our relationships, more than anything else, as a vehicle for developing our personalities.

Your Emotional Quintessence

Our personalities are what we understand to be our own unique individual human nature. Your personality is the sum of your history and all the attributes, attitudes, habits, and experiences that have shaped you. It's what you think of as yourself.

Our personalities are shaped by everything and everyone. Your particular personality is the interaction of your inherited nature with all the things that you went through in childhood, including all the words, touches, nods of the head, caresses, spankings, ignorings, and celebrations of your parents, your encounters with your brothers and sisters, aunts and uncles, neighbors and cousins. Your teachers and playmates also helped shape your personality through all the ways they chided you or praised you, shunned you or begged you to be on their team. It was further developed through all the events of your life, whether tragedies or comedies, mysteries or cheap thrills.

Your personality is a consequence of everything in your environment, and all the things you interact with, mountains and treetops, crayons and video games, farm fields or sixth-floor walk-up apartments. Your personality is "you." It's your personal core.

Your personality is also your emotional quintessence. It's

the way you feel about things: the weather, the sound of the freeway, the national debt, war, your parents, the man you went out with last Friday night, God, butterflies, the singing of birds, and your future. It's the mysterious psychological seismograph that tells you about what you're feeling, when you're happy or well, what hurts your heart or tickles your fancy, when you're in love, what you can't stand, what you believe you can't live through—or without. It's a secret inner photograph of yourself, a map of your own unique emotional terrain. It is your life's energy in motion and it's what makes you distinct from all the other human beings on earth. It's the "one in five billion" ingredient in the recipe of humanity that makes you exactly, precisely, and unrepeatedly—you. But as all-encompassing and ever-present as it is, your personality is also invisible, untouchable, magnetic, powerful, and mysterious.

Our personalities are what we have in common, because each one of us has one—no matter how boring, tyrannical, sweet, mischievous, hateful, overpowering, or Milquetoastish it may be. In short, your personality is you, and so far as most of us know, our personalities are us.

The Personality's Quest

Our personalities don't just lie there like sleeping dogs on the front porches of our lives. They have a program. It is our personalities that fall in love and want to get married. It is our personalities that hope, long for, and feel disappointed, hurt and angry, or overjoyed. It is our personalities that have a heart, feel attached, and want to live happily ever after.

In sum, our personalities want an emotional life, and all the pleasures and satisfactions the life of emotions can give. The fulfillment of all its emotional needs is the personality's passion. Healing, peace, grace, comfort, security, admiration, and a sense of personal well-being are the personality's quest. Our personalities are powerful; they don't like to give up until they get what they want.

The Personality and Relationships

It is through our personalities that we engage in relationships. We love our relationships. They're one of the things that our personalities live for; they give us a sense of belonging, of connection, of purpose, and of value. It's not just that Freud told us that we need both work and love to be whole human beings; it's that our emotional selves have a longing for the connection and reflection that a relationship provides.

Our relationships affect our personalities profoundly. Like God, they give and take so much from us. They can give us a family and take it away; a home and take it away; a sense of belonging and shatter it to smithereens. As we go through our relationships, we discover things about ourselves that show us that both we and they are much more complicated than we ever imagined. Oh, I see our conflict over money isn't only about you, me, and the credit cards; it's also about how your father lost a fortune in the Depression and my mother never bought anything nice for herself. Or our sexual relationship isn't just about how tired we both are; it's about our fear of actually looking into each other's eyes and seeing a stranger there.

Through our relationships, we meet ourselves—again and again and again. That is because the experiences we have in relationships continually touch off our emotions and show us that, fundamentally, we are emotional beings. Emotional life is what distinguishes us from grasshoppers and elephants. We don't just have experiences; we also have feelings about them. What happens to us affects us, makes us happy or sad, enrages or delights us. And it is how we are affected moment by moment *emotionally* which, more than anything else, can reveal ourselves to us. As we react and overreact to people, things, and situations—success and failure, criticism and praise—we gradually get a map of our inner emotional selves. We discover where and how we've been hurt and where, as a consequence, we're incredibly frail or compensatingly mean because of what once happened to us.

It is our acquaintance with our emotions that also points us to the spiritual. Emotions—which are mysterious and can't be exactly measured or weighed—show us that we must be more than just the material substance of our bodies or what we're doing in our lives. Our emotions keep affecting us. We can feel fine one minute and then be in the depths of depression ten minutes later because of something that happened to us. Bad news, a physical pain, somebody's death, the phone call that never comes, getting fired or breaking up, can all ruin a day—or a decade. Our emotions are a kind of daily introduction to the life of the spirit because we are so profoundly affected by them, and yet we can't see them or touch them; we know they aren't "us," but still they're running our lives. And through them, unwittingly, we develop a passing acquaintance with the deeper dimension of our spirits.

It is because we are emotional beings that our relationships are so terribly important to us. It is in our relationships above all, where our feelings are aroused and we feel so deeply, that we also enact our emotions most intensely. Our relationships are the crowning glory of our emotional lives. That is because together, *in relationship,* we go through experiences that show us who we are, how we are broken, and how we need to be mended.

Emotional Wounds

We all had imperfect childhoods in which we were emotionally wounded. Some of our wounds are gaping and grizzly and obvious, and some are so subtle that even the person who's suffered them can barely perceive their true dimension.

Our wounds are the consequence of the imperfect parenting that is an unavoidable fact of the human condition. No family is perfect. No parents do a perfect job of parenting, no matter how well intended, gracious, or loving they may be. No matter how much we try to deny or imagine that we weren't wounded—we all were. And in our hearts, we each secretly recognize that our lives are a symphony of both painful and beautiful notes combined. We have been loved enough to survive, but not enough to feel whole. It is the tragic yet unavoidable failure of family life that invites us to the particular process of growth and resolution that becomes our life's psychological work.

Our relationships awaken us to our true emotional condition. One way or another they keep presenting us with reminders of the people, feelings, and experiences of childhood and show us where we are suffering. They invariably touch us at points of beauty and pain, and keep calling us into the realm of our feelings. Moving through these feelings—the ones we remember and the new ones that arise in relationship—is how we discover our emotional wounds and unmet needs. This is the personality's exquisite labor of love and healing.

The Personality's Healing Journey

As a consequence of our wounds, each of us has a great raft of emotional needs. Many we know; others remain invisible in the murky swamps of the unconscious, waiting to surface when some relationship event stimulates them. But we all have the need to be touched, to be held, to feel whole, respected, and worthy; to be admired and listened to, to be sexually acknowledged. We need to be taken seriously, to be taken passionately, to be treated, in one or a hundred ways, better than our parents treated us. We want to have happy emotional experiences and we want the person with whom we are in a relationship to take us seriously as a suffering, feeling being, so that we can achieve a sense of emotional balance and well-being.

Since the personality's goal in any intimate relationship is to have all our emotional needs met, we all come to our relationships like hungry beggars, saying, if not out loud, then in an unconscious whisper, "What are you going to do for me? Will you fix me? Will you hear me? Are you going to make me feel good? Make my dreams come true? Are you going to be the perfect parent to our children? The father my father wasn't to me, the mother my mother never was? Now that I've fallen in love with you, your job is to make my sorrows vanish. Hear me, fix me, make me feel better." This is the desperate, wounded personality crying out.

There are two levels of emotional needs that we're trying to have met in our intimate relationships. One is the level we're aware of: make me happy, give me financial security; be a good father to our children. The other is that of the unconscious emotional needs that represent our personality's drive to heal whatever stands in the way of our capacity to feel whole.

So it is that in every relationship there is a hidden emotional journey. Being in proximity to another person always changes us, always tells us something about ourselves. But being in an intimate relationship is like an engraved invitation, inviting us to develop. "Look," says the person who shows up, "how about being a little more like me and a little less like your old wounded self? Change a little. Expand, why don't you?"

None of this is actually said out loud, of course. It is quietly expressed, teased in through the process of the relationship itself—the way the tree in the forest gladly falls because someone is watching. But we constantly model ourselves after and are remodeled by one another, through the behaviors and frictions we share—in relationship. Just as children evolve from one stage of development to another—from crawling to walking to learning to thinking to reading, skipping rope, playing hopscotch, going to college, falling in love—adults, too, are constantly evolving, moving through ever-advancing stages of psychological development.

This evolution occurs in our relationships because we're intuitively drawn to the person who has what we don't have, what we lost, what got hurt, or was never developed in childhood. And we establish a relationship with someone and stay connected to that person because we want to develop that missing component in ourselves.

Sometimes this unconscious drive toward wholeness lies in making obvious changes: losing weight, giving up alcohol, changing careers, and sometimes it expresses itself in the realm of the intangible transformations—for example, developing a sense of self-esteem, that mysterious sense that we're okay. But whatever the nature of the changes—claiming your own sexuality, your beauty, intelligence, emotional sensitivity, or artistic talent; learning to love your body; learning how to cry, to dance, to play; or conversely, learning how to put down the yoke of responsibility—all these emotional transformations bring us closer to the fullness of ourselves.

As a result of falling in love, being in relationship, experiencing ourselves in proximity to another person, and sharing a life with him or her, we are becoming all sorts of different things. For example, you may quit smoking, confront your brother about an unresolved conflict, get a law degree, eat better, start meditating, buy a new car, feel good about your flabby thighs, or get over your fear of flying.

Whatever the change, your relationship is changing you, because we are all in an evolutionary process. Something is always becoming of us. We're growing up and getting healed. These changes, which represent a piece of personal development, are what a relationship gives us through the undercurrent of its vitality and its movement through our lives.

This drive to heal and grow is the unconscious mechanism that is always operating in our relationships. We "fall in love," and feel an emotional attraction to the person who can address our unconscious, emotional needs. That "recognition" occurs because of his or her similarity to one of the characters in our childhood dramas: usually father, mother, or siblings.

For example, your father was a spendthrift, endlessly buying new gadgets and tools. And now the man you've fallen in love with, who was always so generous on your dates, turns out to have a money management problem, too. He's always in debt, borrowing money from you. Or your mother was an obsessive housekeeper. She kept everything as neat as a pin—including you. And now, the woman you've married, who was casual and easygoing in her own apartment, turns out, in the house that you share, to be such a fanatic about her clothes, her makeup, and everything that you own that you end up moving all your most precious possessions to a file drawer in your downtown office.

Sooner or later these surprising similarities bring up our emotional pain and insist that we deal with our real feelings about them. Thus, the little girl abused by her father's financial irresponsibilities may finally end up screaming at her lover, "You're just like my father; I'm going to leave if you buy one more useless screwdriver." And the man whose over-controlling mother violated his privacy may say to his wife, "It's so painful to have you always meddling with my things that if you don't stop, someday I'll have to leave."

Life Themes

These points of emotional sensitivity are all stimulated by what I call our life themes. A life theme is a kind of haunted, repetitive chord that keeps playing, at one volume or another, throughout our lives. Everyone has a life theme, originating from some excruciating difficulty you experienced in childhood which then becomes a locus of pain around which the concentric circles of your agonies of a lifetime are drawn. Prominent life themes include: neglect, abuse, abandonment, parental overinvolvement, invisibility, and emotional deprivation. The theme is created in childhood and is reenacted in one or more adult relationships. For example, the man who was beaten by his father becomes a wife beater; the woman whose father was an alcoholic marries two alcoholics, one gambler, and a compulsive eater. The woman whose physician father never came home because he was always at the hospital gets involved with a happy-go-lucky student who soon becomes a workaholic lawyer.

Sometimes the way the themes play themselves out is mysteriously eerie. I know a man whose father was sick his whole life and died when he was fifty-three, and his daughter, born with cerebral palsy, was sick *her* whole life and died when *the man* was fifty-three. Then there's the woman who was abandoned at seven because her mother died, who ended up, because of her divorce, abandoning her own daughter when she was seven. And a friend of mine who became the parent to her two siblings at age ten because her mother was a drunk married a man who's divorced and, due to the death of his ex-wife, she ended up raising his two children.

We don't seek out these mysterious repetitions, they find us. But one way or another, we keep reenacting the dramas of our life themes in order to understand them, to get the messages they are sending, to learn the lessons they are trying to teach. They are what shows us that we are wounded. They teach us that we have feelings. They encourage us—through how we both do and do not receive, respond, and react to them—to learn how to love.

When she was young, my daughter had a book she loved about a blind child and his guide dog, which she kept reading over and over again. It got to be a joke between us. "How many times have you read it now?" I'd ask her, and she'd say, "Six" or "Seventeen" or "Twenty-three." She finally stopped at the twenty-fourth reading. She read it because she loved the story, but also because she was trying to receive its meaning, to understand, for herself, the mystery of blindness, the miracle of a dog's love and loyalty. Finally, when she had apprehended it truly, she put down the book and moved on to other things.

In a similar fashion, we're all trying to apprehend our own histories, to understand what happened to us so that we can finally lay down the books of our early lives and move on to other things. We become able to do this—as my daughter did with her story—by repeating, revisiting, reenacting the scene of the crime. Each time we seek to have our needs met in an adult, romantic relationship, we either *do* get our needs met—and so can put down the books of our childhoods—or, having once again been unable to get them met, feel the emotions that as children we were never able to feel. Finally we can arrive at the awareness of what actually happened to us, feel the anger and sorrow, and, in time, melt into the forgiveness that allows us to leave our childhoods behind.

Whatever the nature of your childhood violations, they represent a theme which you will spend a lifetime identifying, coming to terms with, and transcending. That's because we are all struggling to be whole; and in all of our relationships it is our wholeness that is crying out for recognition.

We are always trying to solve the puzzles our life themes represent; to unlock their mysteries, to come home to the hearth of ourselves. And it is through our intimate relationships that we are given an exquisite opportunity to name, unravel, and heal the anguish of our past.

The wonderful thing is that through our relationships we are actually being healed, reborn, renewed, revamped at the level of our personalities. At the end of our tour of duty in *any* relationship, we have progressed in some inner or outer way in the resolution of our life themes.

That's because our adult relationships bring us into the presence of love. In so doing, they remind us how much we want to be loved, how love is our true condition, and how deeply we hurt when we're not loved well. All relationships can do this to one degree or another, but an intimate relationship where we "fall in love," where there is a sexual bond and the promise of a future, provides us, like no other, with an extraordinary psychological opportunity. Here we can discover how we were wounded, and in these relationships we can also unleash the chains and remove the thorns of our woundedness. For each of us, this is the unimaginable gift of a relationship.

The Limitations of Love at the Personality Level

Despite the beauty of this healing journey and all the emotional changes we're actually able to make, when the personality is the sole definer of our relationships, they invariably disappoint us. That's because the personality is voracious, and wants all of its needs met all of the time; as a result, it expects any relationship to provide perfect happiness.

But, of course, it follows that any expectation this grandiose will likely become the difficulty around which the collapse of the relationship will eventually constellate. The belief that we can get all our emotional needs met by a single other person is invariably followed by disappointment as we discover that this *is* not and *will* not be the case. This extravagant desire in itself can become the reason our relationships go sour.

If you don't believe this, listen to what people say to each other when they're fighting. "You don't meet my needs," they say. "You don't make me feel good. You haven't made me happy. You never take me out to dinner or bring me flowers. You never talk to me. Our sex life is rotten. We never have any fun."

These complaints represent just a tiny sampling from the vast catalogue of needs that the personality expects to be continuously met in a relationship. At the deeper level, what the unsatisfied husband, sweetheart, or lover is actually saying is "You haven't been the perfect replacement parent, you haven't delivered me from the pain of my childhood. You haven't met all my emotional needs, i.e., this relationship isn't perfect, and so I'm out of here."

As personalities, we continue to hope and believe that our emotional selves will be totally fulfilled by our intimate relationships. This belief is so strong, so deeply ingrained, and so pervasive in society that, as a consequence, naturally it generates a highly exaggerated sense of self-importance. This self-focus is our attempt, by God, to squeeze perfect happiness out of our intimate relationships.

Overly Involved Self-Focus

Because our relationships have come to promise fulfillment of the emotional self, they can't help but launch us into a state of self-focus which is very narcissistic. By narcissistic, I mean presuming that everyone else is exactly like you and seeing the whole world as revolving around you and your needs—rather than recognizing the uniqueness of each individual and seeing the world as a place in which everyone is in need. People with an overly involved self-focus are so desperate to get their own needs met that they can never see the other person in a relationship for who he or she is.

For example, there's the successful businessman who never received his father's approval and expects his wife, his secretary, his employees, the parking lot attendant, and the maître d' all to bow to his every need. The folks who encounter him feel run over, invisible, and worthless in their own right. Or the woman whose cool, disapproving mother could never confirm her femininity, and who as a consequence expects—sometimes through screaming hysterical outbursts—that her husband, her father-in-law, and every other man on the face of the earth will tell her she's beautiful, buy her flowers, listen ad infinitum to her every tale of woe, and satisfy her every other whim. The men who have been related to her feel eviscerated, powerless, and desperate because they can never make her happy.

All of us suffer from narcissism to one degree or another because, of course, none of our parents could perfectly meet all our needs and, as we have seen, at the personality level our quest is precisely to find a way to satisfy all of them. As a result we do a lot of projecting of our needs and desires onto the people we love in hopes that they will fulfill them: I love chocolate; you must love it, too. I like to make love in the afternoon; of course you'll want to also. I love dogs; let's get ten.

But, in fact, our partners are completely different from us and have their own sets of needs, wounds, and expectations. Most of us can't see that; instead we keep constantly mistaking our partners for ourselves in the hope that if they are exactly like us, we'll finally get what we want. We continue to imagine and assume that our sweethearts, lovers, husbands, and wives will want what we want, feel what we feel, and as a result behave exactly like we do. We drown them with our needs and expectations; we wear ourselves out with our exhausting quest for emotional fulfillment.

Since our needs feel so immense, we simply can't let up.

The tragedy is that when we endlessly project onto our partners, a relationship becomes an engagement in which two people, both desperately trying to be seen, can only see their own reflection. They can't see the other person at all.

Since all this is being asked of one relationship, it's no wonder that the unfinished narcissistic business of childhood becomes an incredibly grueling undertaking. At its highest level, any relationship could be a sacred temple of true vision or a place of divine curiosity where we love a person who is totally different from ourselves. But when narcissism comes into play, a relationship often becomes the pool in which, because of endlessly bending over and trying to see our own reflection, we finally drown.

The truth is that emotional needs can never be fully satisfied; they are an endlessly revolving kaleidoscope, ravenous, insatiable, and huge. Moving beyond them is the only way to ensure that they won't devour us whole.

Beyond Narcissism

The sad thing about our narcissistic self-focus is that it puts a terrible burden on our relationships. The beautiful thing about it is that hopefully—through our earnest endeavor to be satisfied at the personality level, to fulfill all our needs—we gradually discover, if we're paying attention, that this can't possibly happen. It is precisely in awakening to the emotional limitations of our relationships that we begin to seek further: "Ah, you can't make me perfectly happy," we say, "and yet, surprise, I still love you. Maybe relationships are really more about love than just getting my needs met." "Oh, so you won't spend all your time and energy making me feel good; maybe I should look inwardly, deeply. Perhaps I should meditate, take my mind off myself. Perhaps I should talk to God. Perhaps I should make my view of the world a little bit larger. In that world I see that, like me, other people, too, are suffering. Perhaps I should think of serving them, instead of being so focused on myself."

All these whisperings are the voice of the soul inside us, teasing us toward a higher awareness, a grander view of love than the search for emotional fulfillment. Frustrations awaken us; the limitations of our relationships invite us to evolve. For no matter how hard we try, no matter how many times we go over and over our emotional issues, we can never be perfectly satisfied, we can never be completely healed. We never attain perfect union.

Our dissatisfaction gives us a choice: we can hold on, stamp our feet, and demand to be pleased at the personality level, or, precisely because of our endless frustration, we can decide to expand, to respond to the call of the soul, to move toward the further reaches of love.

Chapter 4

A Higher
Calling

Relationships as an
Expression of the Soul

Being human is ultimately a journey of spiritual evolution. In Western culture until now, this has taken the form of the development of psychological consciousness. We have wanted to know who we are and how we got to be this way. In particular, we have wanted to solve the emotional riddles laid out by our families by individuating ourselves from the clutches of those families, and by identifying and putting to good use our unique human potentials.

The psychotherapist has been the guru in these areas, instructing the "patient" in discovering what he feels, midwifing him through the resolution of his childhood feelings, and finally, helping him to find work and establish relationships that satisfy his emotional needs with some degree of consciousness. All these undertakings have been engaged in at the psychological level; we have pursued them for pleasure, amusement, and satisfaction, and also for the process of emotional clearing.

This journey of psychological healing and self-discovery has been the path to personal evolution and enlightenment in our culture. It is out of these pursuits and sets of values that we have developed our relationships and ourselves as personalities.

As we have seen, however, our relationships have neither stayed within their familiar formats nor have they brought us the level of satisfaction that allows us to completely rest in them. We still have discomfort; we find ourselves in excruciating relationship predicaments; our relationships falter and end, and it is all this discomfort, interestingly enough, that has made way for the agenda of the soul.

The Soul's Agenda

The soul is the divine fragment within us. It is the light in our eyes, the energy in the breath we breathe. The soul is eternal, out of time, a commodity of the spiritual realm, the one great vast umbrella or pool of light of which we are all an individual piece.

The individual soul is a bit of spiritual uniqueness—cosmic DNA—that is particular to each person who possesses it. Just as a personality follows a particular path, an evolution it is pursuing, so does the soul.

The soul has interests that are different from those of the personality. The soul is not so interested in what a person can amass, collect, or achieve within a given lifetime, as it is in having us develop an awareness of our eternal radiant and beautiful nature, inviting us to remember the oneness of which we are all a part.

The soul isn't interested in marriage—or any other relationship for that matter—except as it allows a person to become more aware of his or her own soul. The soul is interested in every life experience, whether wonderful or ugly, easy or excruciating, that awakens us. The soul allows us to see that the experiences of this life are merely pictures in a photo album which also contains the photographs of other dimensions.

In the evolution of human consciousness, the personality is like the self-seeking child, while the soul is the seasoned, wise adult. The personality has simple wants: the desire for the pleasures and habits of human life. The soul has the generosity of a vast awareness. The highest, grandest part of our being, the soul is larger than life because it survives beyond life. It is the eternal part of us all; it is our essence, the mysterious absence we recognize in the body that is no longer alive. We all have this essence. It is without form or substance. It is seamless and faceless, and each one of our souls is a smidgen of the vast grand whole that is all our souls wrapped into one. We started out together as one; life is our little detour until we go back to that one.

The soul is love, it is the energy, the beauty and eternity of pure love. It is our essence. There is no other.

The Soul and Intimate Relationships

As it pertains to our relationships, the soul is the invisible force that is driving them from a different vantage point—and toward different ends—than the personality. In the small human frame of daily experience, we enter into relationships to promote the outcomes that the personality desires: a warm body to wake up next to, a Friday movie date, someone to bear your children or to fix the roof. But, as we have seen, there is a profound frustration in this emotional undertaking because it doesn't account for the whole of the picture.

That's because, although we think of ourselves exclusively as personalities, we are also souls. And just as the values of marriage and society are interwoven in our relationship lives, so also our souls and personalities are beautifully interwoven in them. Together soul and psyche are always moving us forward, each in quest of its own evolution.

Our focus on our emotionally driven psychological selves is the reason why our relationships have evolved in the way that they have, why we have "worked on" them so much, why we have expected so much from them. We have considered the personality to be the whole of our personal selves, and consequently, have elevated our relationships to the level of an absolute. Why, we've practically worshipped them like a god. Engaging in them with only a portion of our essence—our personalities—we have expected that somehow they would satisfy our spiritual selves as well. This, of course, they have been unable to do.

It's not that our souls have been absent in our relationships.

It is, rather, that they have been submerged, somewhere off-screen, out of focus, not at the forefront of how we've been conducting our relationships. And so, although at many points along our relationship paths the soul presents us with its challenges, we have tended to see our issues merely as personality problems and tried to solve them only at that level.

The truth is that our souls and personalities are always operating simultaneously in our relationships, but our souls, because they have been denied and held in abeyance so long, are now insisting that we pay attention to the overwhelmingly powerful role they play in our relationships. To that end, they are presenting us with more and more invitations to encounter our spiritual selves at their highest capacity for love.

This call is being sounded now because, as a species, we are standing at the brink of a larger spiritual awareness that is already quietly infiltrating our consciousness. But it is also because our personalities have been satisfied to some degree, and are now willing to raise the spiritual questions that were, in fact, there all along.

The psyche and spirit always work hand in hand; each using the opportunities that the other creates. Each emotional wound is an opportunity to move to the spiritual level; each moment of spiritual awakening a chance to move toward greater emotional maturity. So it is, for example, that the lover, betrayed, can be self-righteous on the emotional level, or through the searing pain of betrayal can move toward the larger spiritual frame of forgiveness, seeing himself or herself as just one of many who have been wounded in this way. Similarly, the person whose spirit is generous and kind and may imagine that these virtues are sufficient to a relationship,

may need to learn how to take on the homely emotional responsibilities of daily chores or how to negotiate about sex, a
vacation, or a movie date.

In every intimate encounter, the soul as well as the personality is being invited to grow. How the soul extends these
invitations to growth can be seen most clearly through the
readily identifiable stages of an intimate relationship.

The Stages of an Intimate Relationship

No matter what its particular form, every intimate relationship
goes through seven distinct emotional and spiritual stages or
stations of the cross. Whether we get through all of them or
recycle through just the first few of them in every subsequent
relationship is the measure of whether we are allowing the
soul to do its work on us. In each relationship, we are given
the opportunity to move through all seven stages and to be
affected by the spiritual dimension of love until we are transformed and move to a higher level of loving.

When we embark upon a relationship, we don't expect or
imagine that this will be our journey, but it will be—at least
as far as we're willing to go. According to the cherished
myths of marriage, we just fall in love and live happily ever
after; but falling in love is just the first stop on the train. Once
you've bought a ticket, you're in for a ride.

These seven stages are the benchmarks of every relationship, whether it's a fifty-year marriage, a two-year gay relationship, or a year-long weekend romance.

We all go through the relationship grind. We just don't
know that we do, or that it's inescapable. To become aware

that there is, in fact, a predictable psychospiritual process we're all going through is liberation in itself. It isn't a requirement of having a good or a bad relationship. It just happens anyway, but to the degree that we do become conscious of it, we can become much kinder to ourselves as we go through all the steps. Instead of beating ourselves up, which is the usual human instinct, we can enter the journey as a teaching, with compassion for ourselves. In time, we will also see that it is the larger, much more profound energy of the soul that is driving all our intimate relationships. To the degree that we can acknowledge this, we can allow each relationship to become a vehicle for the raising of our consciousness.

1. Romance: Moonlight and Red Roses

In any relationship, we first have the experience that we commonly call "falling in love." This is the moment of ineffable, mystical attraction, which flows into the season of courtship and romance. This is the part of the story where you fall in love and act out all the emotional, hormonal, psychological experiences that draw you into a passionate soul connection. If you're lucky, it will be punctuated by moonlight and red roses, some candlelight dinners, perhaps even a lovely vacation or two.

When we fall in love, we feel wonderful, beautiful, magical, invincible. We're optimistic; we're sexually and emotionally thrilled. We're cataloguing our hopes for the future. We have an ecstatic, transcendent experience, and it is the sublime caliber of that experience which makes us willing to risk taking on a relationship; the dimensions of real and ordinary daily life, with another human being. Because it is so romantic, so charming, this stage of intimate relations is a story you'll love to remember.

While we're falling in love and having this delicious experience, we say to ourselves, "I've found the person of my dreams; everything's going to be wonderful. We'll have a beautiful future." This is the personality talking. The personality is having a heyday. It thinks that, finally, at last, it's going to get all of its needs met.

The soul, meanwhile, in some quiet corner, knows that this choice is being made for another reason, one that won't necessarily make all our personality dreams come true. It is offering the two people who fall in love a momentary glimpse of what real love looks like, inviting them to hold on to that glimpse through all the challenges to come.

2. Commitment: The Pledge

The second stage is commitment. It may be referred to as a marriage, because whether this second stage is in fact a garden variety heterosexual marriage, a gay marriage, a second marriage or living together in a marriage clone, it is *some* form of commitment. There's some sort of conscious acknowledgment that a relationship exists and is going to be pursued. Some kind of pledge—a marriage vow or simply an agreement to continue seeing one another on Saturday evenings—is made that acknowledges this.

In this phase, our romantic expectations are off and running. We'll live in Seattle, we'll buy that cute little house, we'll vacation in Maine, for our anniversary we'll go on a cruise, we'll join the athletic club. Maybe we'll rent a cottage on the lake for the summer. Bob and Carol will be our best friends. We'll have your mom and dad over for Thanksgiving dinner. We'll be together, we'll have some children or pets, and we'll live happily ever after.

This is the part of the story where our emotional selves write the scenario, where we imagine that every emotional need will finally be met in grand style. Again, our souls are up to something else, but they are still operating offstage. In spite of bad timing, inconvenience, or absolutely the wrong kind of person, you feel compelled, anyway, to take the step of commitment. So it is that the forty-eight-year-old publicist marries the thirty-two-year-old personal trainer; the man in England plights his troth to the sophomore at UCLA, and the woman in Australia comes to America to marry the divorced father of six she met at a phone booth in Israel during the war. In each of these cases, despite their personality's hesitation, and in some instances outright cry of insanity, the person was responding to the call of his or her soul.

3. Crisis: A Crack in the Vase

At some point in every new relationship, there's always an opening crisis. One person is madly in love and the other has cold feet; there's a problem with a stepchild; there's a death in the family; or a financial struggle; one wants a child or a dog and the other doesn't; a mother-in-law turns out to be a vampire; there's an illness that taxes the mettle of the new lovers; the man offers the woman a gift she refuses—a bracelet she doesn't like, the wrong bottle of perfume, a trip to Costa Rica—his ego is hurt and he starts withdrawing.

Whatever the form of the crisis, there's now a crack in the vase. The relationship has gone through something that reveals to the partners that they are not going to live together in total bliss. It's at this point that the differences between the two people are revealed, suddenly, painfully, through discourse, it becomes clear that they don't, in fact, understand each other perfectly. They're two different people with two distinctly different agendas. Into the realm of love and bliss steps the specter of truth and reality.

However this moment of crisis eventually plays out, it is the first moment of disillusionment. The veils of romantic illusion are lifted and the issue that was raised by the crisis will now become a theme of its own. First, how are the two people who have just fallen in love going to handle the fact that their love isn't perfect? Second, whose way of doing things is going to prevail? Are we going to let your mother live in the house as you want, or not, as I prefer? Are we going to move to Idaho for my great job opportunity or stay in Boston where you already have work?

As each person discovers his or her own nasty feelings about whatever it is that has been revealed, the glossy film of "how love was supposed to be" is gradually drawn back. The personality is disillusioned and now the work of the soul truly begins. We are asked first of all to contain this difficulty in love. Can we still love the person who has turned out to be a mere mortal, who wants something that disappoints us, or, worse yet, who wants to turn our whole life upside down?

Second, we are asked to discern what is the larger meaning of this. Will we grow through surrendering to the conflict, the unwanted agenda, the unthinkable revelation? Or are our souls, precisely through the issue that has been raised, urging us to clarify our own values? "I won't move to Idaho so you can run a gambling casino; I'm staying here to work in the children's AIDS hospice."

4. Ordeal: The Power Struggle

The ordeal is the long, meandering phase of a relationship in which an issue keeps surfacing, apparently unable to be resolved. ("You're stingy, just like my father.") The same fights happen. ("I hate you for being so cheap; you don't love me.") Reconciliations occur. (You kiss and make up.) Awareness grows, understanding develops. ("Now that I understand how poor your family was, I see why you're so careful with your money.") Resentments deepen. ("For God's sake, at least you could buy me some flowers for our anniversary.") Exhaustion gets expressed. ("I'm fed up, we've been married six years and you have yet to bring me a box of candy.") And so does outrage. ("You *are* just like my father and I'm not going to do this one more minute.")

The ordeal is the developmental process of your life themes at work. Here lie all the events and experiences by which you will discover your differences, work them through one way or another, and develop some aspect of your personality that was submerged or needed development. However it is initiated, emotional issues are presented to the partners in an endless kaleidoscopic array insisting upon change.

The ordeal is always a journey of intense emotional growth. It is invariably a power struggle because the energies of our personalities are invested in protecting us from feeling pain. If you were abandoned, for example, you will do anything, bring all your powers—nice or nasty—to bear in a desperate endeavor not to feel abandoned again. If your partner was abused by an overinvolved, overpossessive parent, he or she will do the same—marshal all his energies, straight out or passive-aggressively—to try to prevent you from making him feel that way ever again. When the ordeal becomes exquisite and thorny, instead of exploring yourself, it's easy to become defensive and self-righteous, to find your partner or the relationship at fault, which, of course it is, because every relationship is imperfect. "Love just doesn't work," you say. "See, once again, I've married my father."

As the relationship goes through the ordeal, it is no longer being carried along on the wings of romance and great expectations; it is being dragged along by disappointment and disillusion. Why hasn't our love fulfilled our dreams, become the perfect fairy tale we imagined? Why has it, instead, become this monstrosity that's bringing up all our fears and vulnerabilities? At this point, we all have a choice of saying, "Okay, you're not my everything, so I'm out of here." Or of saying, "Oh, I get it, there's an opportunity here. I'm being invited to deal with my own emotional issues, to stop being angry at my father for abandoning me, my mother for smothering me."

At this point you can get stuck in blaming or you can start looking at yourself. If you're courageous, you will respond to the challenge, and if you are steadfast, you may actually move to the place where you are no longer just endlessly slapped around and controlled by your emotions.

Sometimes, what we become as a result of the ordeal is something we always wanted to become, and sometimes it's the last thing in the world that we ever wanted to take on or face. During one of my own relationships, I was given by my partner, a body worker, the gift of health and learned how to eat, drink, and prepare foods that I never before would have contemplated eating. There were tedious and horrible parts of this culinary redemption—a kitchen out of control, old habits to give up, more time spent in learning the exact components of food than I ever wanted to know—but it was, in fact, a gift I wanted to receive. In that same relationship, my partner learned how to cry, something he never wanted to do but was moved and overjoyed to have learned. How we arrived there wasn't easy; we both resisted and clawed—if not at the beginning, then along the way. If not at one another, then at the gods.

In the ordeal phase of a relationship, the partners are called on to face the emotional issues and deal with the life themes that sensitize them. It's at this point that the true emotions of both partners come out in the open: disappointment, rage, hate, envy. The dark side of the personality reveals its murky grandeur. Unconscious expectations are revealed as disappointments are being expressed: "I married you because I thought you were successful and prosperous, but now you've lost your job. How can you do this to me?" Or "I married you because I thought you were kind and tender and understanding. But it turns out that you have a hormonal imbalance and you're a raving, hysterical maniac twenty days of the month." Or "You just wanted children, you don't care about me."

As the power struggle continues, everything starts feeling out of control and the lovers are faced with a choice. They can try to put the relationship back in the box, stamp their feet and pound their fists on the wall, and demand that it fulfill all their expectations on a psychological level—or they can start to grow.

Through its grueling repetitive insistence that we confront our emotional issues, the ordeal also becomes an invitation to the spiritual. It invites us to view our issues in a larger context, to ask why we have to face them in the first place, to consider what they have to teach us. It also invites us to resolve them, so we can stop fixating on them and move on to other things. What would it mean, for example, if you could stop thinking about your abandonment and insisting that every lover on earth not leave you? What would it mean if you could trust that the person you love won't have to suffocate you? What would it mean to stop being so fearful of everything and trust in the goodness of the universe?

Ultimately, this confrontation can open our hearts and bring liberation to our spirits. As each issue dissolves, we move one step closer to love. Each time we resolve an emotional issue, it is no longer there to dog us, to keep us chained to the emotional level. We can start to relax, to let down our guard. The more easy we feel about ourselves, the more generous, expansive, and empathic we can be. These all are the properties of spiritual love.

Furthermore, in order to move past this stage of relationship, we must begin to understand that along with our partner's limitations, flaws, faults, and failings, we have personality imperfections of our own. This introduces us to the realm of forgiveness, one of the highest attributes of spiritual love.

Each time we let go of a psychological issue that has consumed our attention and has been a point of focus in a relationship, our capacity for love—the genuine wholehearted acceptance of another—is expanded. Each time we resolve an emotional issue, we come closer to our spiritual selves. *This is because it is our attachment to our emotional dramas, more than anything else, that keeps us from really being able to love.*

Love is unconditional acceptance; the ordeal is, paradoxically, an invitation to move to that place—to unconditionally accept yourself and the other person. Here's another imperfect person to love, each relationship will say to you. Here's another irritating, immature, frustrating, agonizingly difficult person to help you get beyond your own emotional reactions, and to learn how to simply embrace with love.

It is this process of falling in love, of dreaming of the perfect future, investing in expectations and then having reality—the ordeal—impinge, that can move us to spiritual growth. It is through the ordeal that our relationships can do astonishing things. It is the ordeal itself that gradually moves us toward more perfect and lasting love.

For many of us, this growth to love takes a number of relationships—the dashing of multitudes of dreams and expectations—until we finally surrender to love's higher agenda. The personality doesn't give in easily. It's been invested in having its needs met for our whole lives. It's so cocksure of what a relationship should be that it's only when we've been battered, scathed, and humbled that we're finally willing to give up these notions and truly love.

5. Chaos: Loss of Control

At some point in the ordeal, before resolution arrives, you will undoubtedly descend into the black hole of chaos. Chaos is when you feel as though everything you thought, imagined, expected, and dreamed would happen in your relationship obviously, clearly, has not come to pass and all your efforts during the ordeal have been futile. You're at your wit's end and you don't know which way is up. You have no idea what to do, don't know whether to get out or stay in, call a psychiatrist, put yourself on Prozac, or head for the Golden Gate Bridge and jump headfirst. If all is not lost, it certainly feels like it is. *You* are lost—in the chaos.

Here you come to realize that the issue which has dogged your relationship is gigantic, immense, and irresolvable. Completely out of your control. You perhaps recognize it even more because, as a result of going through the ordeal, you have developed some awareness and capabilities which now make you feel more equipped to be a self and less willing to be an undifferentiated blob, drowning in the pool of the relationship. The arrival of chaos is announced to you or your partner by any one of the following behaviors: an affair, fights that don't end and bring neither resolution nor further growth, boredom, or the awareness that you've grown apart and there's no common ground anymore.

At this point, some people choose marriage counseling, which, unfortunately, in many cases is an endeavor to put the relationship back in the box by "working on" a marriage which is, in fact, already over. Sometimes the chaos is the void from which springs a new beginning. At others, it is a swamp from which THE END of a relationship emerges.

Chaos is yet another invitation to the spiritual level. There's an opportunity here to say, "You've disappointed me; but what is the greater meaning of this agony?" or "What is the greater undertaking of this relationship?" Most of us can't do this at the time. We're too pitched in the battle, too lost in the chaos, too busy holding on to the shreds of our dreams, our convictions about how it ought to be. And yet, this loss of control matures and expands us in spite of ourselves. The agony it delivers on the emotional level throws open a window to the spiritual level.

6. Surrender: The Awakening

Surrender is the spiritual act of giving up, giving way, giving in. When you surrender, you give up your expectations, give way to the process, and give in to what has occurred. It is spiritual because it assumes that a force greater than yourself is guiding the action and will be there to catch you, that you are not alone on the tightrope of your personality without a net.

The minute you have surrendered, light begins to dawn in your relationship. Patterns suddenly emerge that were never visible before. You're able to see that everything you went through, as chaotic and difficult and painful as it was, *did* amount to something. You hoped and expected that one thing would happen—you'd get married, have your two point five children, and live happily ever after. But as a matter of fact, what happened was that through all the conflicts—all those bloody fights about money, whether or not to have children, or to move to Florida—you gained the emotional strength that you never before had possessed.

You also discovered that there was a purposefulness and continuity to what occurred—that as a matter of fact, the ordeal was very specific in its demands on you. One day when you were in the impossible situation you thought you couldn't bear for another minute, you rose up and found your voice and for the first time in your life spoke up for yourself. And then, when your darling persisted in the behavior that had always driven you crazy, you found your voice once again and spoke up again, until finally, something in you was developed that had never been there before.

Or you wanted your wife never to abandon you. You married her because she gave you that wonderful feeling of security. But the minute the two of you were married, she became so secure that she decided to take some risks. She joined a few clubs, went back to school, made some new friends, and so instead of being cozy at home with you every night over the soup bowl, she was gone day after day, making you feel— that's right—abandoned again. And what did you learn in the process? You became strong in the face of your abandonment. You screamed and yelled at her and told her she had too many friends, too many engagements, too many things to do, and then finally *you* developed new friends, other interests, an emotional expansiveness you never would have found if she had knuckled under to your demands.

The awakening is that time in a relationship when we see the true purpose of the ordeal. We are psychologically illumined about what has been occurring and we're finally able to see that a pattern beyond our conventional perception was there, quietly operating, all the time. Something has become of us. We recognize this. We're not sure exactly what it is, it's something different, something we didn't necessarily or particularly want to be, but here we are, born anew. As we break through these psychological limitations, we clear the space in which our souls can blossom.

7. Transformation: True Love

After the ordeal, chaos, and surrender comes transformation. The person—and the situation—have been forever changed. In transformation, we thoroughly integrate the growth that has occurred. The strength you've developed becomes your own; the tragedy you've lived through loses its power to emotionally derail you. You are now a person who contains emotional and spiritual attributes which before, you did not possess. Having gone through all the psychospiritual stages of a relationship, you have now arrived at an entirely different level from where you were when you entered it.

This transformation means that you've become something, developed something, become much more of your soul's self as a result of this process of relationship. Not only has this particular change become an irrevocable part of you, but in some larger sense you have grown a new personality; you have walked closer to your soul. From this time on, you will be different. Just as physical growth can't be measured during the exact moments when it is occurring, so, too, emotional and spiritual growth mysteriously creeps up on us. Last year, you were five feet six inches tall, but as a result of a spurt of growth, you're now five feet nine. You think you're just plodding along, that every day is the same and nothing is changing. Then one day you wake up and discover that, lo and behold, you're no longer afraid of being stupid, or that, miraculously, you do feel good about yourself. You have acquired that weird psychological commodity, a sense of self-esteem, or you're at peace with your sexuality. What's beautiful about transformation is that it is absolute, a one-way street. You can never go back to the way you were.

By the time we arrive at this place of transformation, we are, of course, bloodied and wearied from the journey, from all the effort, control, denial, disappointment, agony, disbelief, hope, yearning, misery, emotional, and spiritual violence that has occurred along the way. The transformation that arises is precious; it is dearly bought and paid for, and maybe by now you're so sick of the person who unwittingly put you through all this personal evolution that, now transformed, you want to just pick up your marbles and go home to somebody else. A great many people don't make it through this rite of passage with the partner who started out on the journey with them. Indeed, it is at this point precisely that many relationships break apart. You've completed your emotional task—whatever it was, you're ready for the next level of development—and perhaps a new partner to shepherd you through it.

Of course, one of the choices after you have been transformed is to end the relationship. A grander possibility is that both of you have been changed in such a way that the relationship itself has changed—evolved—and can begin or continue on another level. You have finally learned how to be empathic; she doesn't have to have an affair to crowbar you into getting in touch with your feelings; she's finally learned she's intelligent; she doesn't have to compete with you in every conversation. Through the agony of the ordeal, you have become visible, whole, real, three-dimensional to one another.

This is a moment of great emotional resolution and spiritual fulfillment.

I know a couple who lived through eighteen years of the wife's infidelity with another man—her answer to her husband's workaholic ways. When this woman finally brought her affair to the surface, because their children were grown and she was ready to leave her husband for her lover, he pleaded for her to stay, to talk, to go through his pain with him. Week by week, together, they dealt with all the emotional issues. Thread by thread, they unraveled the feelings they'd never expressed, the pain, the love, the sorrow, the points along their path when they'd each abandoned the other. For the first time in their marriage, they spoke the truth to one another. The honesty of their ordeal became the fuel of renewed and deepened sexual passion. They fell in love in a way that they never had before, a love born of transparency and deep feeling. This woman said goodbye to her lover, recommitted to her husband, and for six years now they have been living a breathtakingly conscious marriage in which the habit of speaking the truth that they developed in crisis has become the hallmark of their every interaction.

Transformation requires either that you live in your current relationship at a new level that incorporates the growth you have both now integrated—dovetailing in some new and elevated fashion. Or that, because of the agonies or the incompatibilities that have developed as a consequence of all that growth, you leave the relationship and proceed to the next level with someone else.

Either way, transformation is just another word for nothing left to lose. You didn't get your way. Your relationship wasn't perfect. You had to face your own imperfections. You lost control. For a minute there—or a year or two—you thought you were losing your mind. Finally, you gave up, and as at the end of a bad dream, you woke up and found out that you were still alive.

This is the moment of the miracle. Whether or not the relationship continues, you see the whole picture, the whole person. You have been released from the power struggle, from the endless fixation on all your petty, gigantic, emotional grievances. And when you have moved from the attachment of the personality level and arrived at the detachment that is real love, you have been truly transformed.

The highest level of this transformation, which may take decades and many partners to achieve, or may never be fulfilled in a single lifetime, is reached when we are able simply to embrace another person with nothing but the grace of pure love, with total perception, total reception, total acceptance. The ultimate goal of all our relationship experiences is to deliver us to this place of pure love—no judgment, no ax to grind, no needs to whimper over or insist on being fulfilled. Just love. Pure love.

A Spiritual Invitation

I recently met a couple at the airport. They were going off on a tropical vacation and they were both beaming. The woman told me they'd been married thirty years. "Twenty of them were awful," she said. "We disagreed about everything; we both threatened to leave a hundred times. But by now, we've had all the fights that the two of us could have about the five or six issues we will always disagree on. We both know our positions; we both know we're not going to change. We've decided to accept each other—to love each other, you might say. We're going to Tahiti, and I know we'll have a wonderful time."

This couple was able to reach this place together. Some people, however, enter that stage of transcendence to the spiritual level only when their relationships have ended. For example, I recently met a man who told me a story about spending the weekend with his former wife on the occasion of one of their children's graduation from law school. He said, "I fell in love with her thirty years ago and I loved her for all the quirky, weird things that were unique about her. I was married to her for twenty years and eventually, those things became irritating as hell to me, and finally were the reason I divorced her. Now that I'm divorced from her, I find myself being able to appreciate those things all over again. I guess you could say that once again, though differently, I've fallen in love with her."

As this story demonstrates, the great spiritual message of the journey of our intimate relationships is that there is no ultimate satisfaction on the personality level. We can move in and out of appreciation. We can be irritated and struggle with irreconcilable differences. There is temporary satisfaction, even delight. We will have sweetness, beautiful moments, and all the comforts of home. But we will never have perfection. The person you love will never be quite perfect and even the most beautiful relationship you can create will have its limitations. No matter how much you balk, scream, or try to train the imperfect person you love, he or she will never change enough to fulfill your image of perfection. And the lovely but imperfect relationship will never be perfect enough to be worshipped like a god. All this imperfection is calling us to love. To love the person just as he is and the situation exactly as it unfolds. But only when we've used up all our tricks and worn ourselves out on the personality level will we finally be able to comprehend the meaning of the agony.

This journey through the stations of the cross is nothing less than a spiritual initiation. At each critical juncture we have a choice: we can stay fixated on the personality level, stranded with the agenda of fulfilling our needs; or we can respond to the invitation and move to a higher level of love. We can expand our hearts; we can move from attachment to a particular outcome to the acceptance of a whole person; we can give up our psychological agendas and surrender to the journey.

Through the high windows of the crisis, ordeal, chaos, and transformation, we can glimpse an illumination of our spiritual selves. And through the whole process, we can actually leave behind a bit of our healed, transformed personalities and step just a little bit more into our spiritual selves. In this way, through the journey of our intimate relationships, we are escorted ever onward to the spiritual level of love.

Chapter 5

The Journey to the Future

Relationships and the Development of Spiritual Consciousness

The soul is a vast entity. It is the container of all containers. Its mission is gathering, melting, unifying. Its purpose isn't to make us aware of our individuality or our uniqueness. Nor does it want to make us aware of the wounds and insults to our particular egos and restore them to fatness. Its purpose, rather, is to show us that there is something larger, more beautiful than the individual and to invite us, in radiance, to become a part of it. The agenda of the soul, then, is to move us from focused individual awareness to a melting diffused awareness of our truly unified state. The soul does this in a beautiful orderly way.

When, as children, we left our individual families to enter the world, we gradually discovered our similarities to other human beings. We found out that they, too, had mothers and fathers, TV sets, dogs and cats, and trouble with their homework. Later, if we continued to pay attention, we discovered that, like us, they also had difficulties with their families and felt weird and lonely down in their little rabbit holes. We moved from insularity—the sense that we were all alone in our individual families—to community—the awareness that our family was one of many going through the typical family experience. We moved from seeing ourselves as the only person in the world trapped in a family drama to the growing awareness that *everyone* in *every* family was going through some difficulties. Gradually, we realized that we all had a few things in common. This realization invited us to make the shift from separateness to a sense of community. In a similar way, the soul invites us to move from a sense of the isolation in our relationship experiences to a larger field of relatedness.

In this progression, for example, you may start out by saying, "My marriage isn't working. What's the matter with me? I feel like a failure, the only person on earth who can't have a good relationship." Then, when your best friend tells you she's filing for divorce, you say, "Oh, I see I'm not the only one." And then, when you read the divorce statistics in the paper, you understand that a lot of people's relationships aren't working. "This must be a phenomenon," you tell yourself. "A lot of people are going through this."

At the other end of the spectrum, you may be having a beautiful love affair and saying to yourself, "Nobody can imagine how wonderful I feel." Then a total stranger tells you that he's just fallen in love and you find yourself saying, "I know exactly how you feel. It's fabulous, isn't it? I'm so excited for you."

Through such experiences, we see that, like ourselves, others have had relationship miracles and tragedies. We see the common thread of our human, romantic experience and we have a momentary experience of unified awareness.

The personality focuses on the particular individual—I, me, mine. The soul focuses on *what the vast collection of individuals hold in common*. The soul is always looking for and driving us toward the bigger picture, the larger container. That is because it is in our souls that we are joined and partake of a common spiritual substance. In our souls, we are each a part of the immense bedrock of spirit, the one big soul of which each of our individual souls are a little beautiful part. So it is that when our relationships bring us to a moment of soul awareness, of what our souls experience in common, we recognize the true magnitude of our relatedness.

As we have seen, at the personality level, we are continually engaged with our emotional lives. We are dragged around by feelings we never intended to have, problems we never knew existed; and we are continually forced to acknowledge the dominating power of our emotions. In this experience, we reluctantly learn that we are not in control. That's the way it was meant to be. The personality entices us into relationships and then introduces us to the disappointments that whet our appetites to seek what we are really looking for. Through the frustration of the personality's quest, we are ushered ever more toward the agenda of the soul. This is the way our relationships move us toward spiritual consciousness.

Spiritual Consciousness

Spiritual consciousness is a unique kind of awareness in which we utterly, absolutely comprehend that we are far more than ordinary people living ordinary human lives. We are, in fact, eternal spirits who have stepped into life with a grand and specific purpose: to be able to love without limitation.

Although many of us have this awareness in a pure form in infancy, it becomes gradually eroded as we take up life in the so-called real world, where we are subjected to the dramas of our family lives. These dramas create our life themes. As a result, we enter into the psychological processes, through which, over time, we endeavor to understand ourselves in order to get back to the pure state of love.

We do this either consciously as fully active participants or as emotionally unconscious sleepwalkers. But however we do it, at some level we are all trying to heal emotionally because the less psychological debris we hold on to, the more spiritually available we become. To put it simply, the more we have done our emotional homework, the more able we are to actually love. This is a tiny opening to spiritual consciousness.

Another way to look at it is that we come into life with open hearts, but the process of living leaves them scarred and encrusted by the time we reach adulthood. Through the labor of love that relationships call us to, we expose our hearts in all their brokenness and through that unveiling in the presence of others, we are offered the opportunity to return to the state of spiritual consciousness, which is pure love.

Another way we can regain spiritual consciousness is

through certain extraordinary life experiences. In these divinely gifted, apparently "supernatural" moments, we suddenly, utterly understand, once again, that we are spiritual beings living human lives. This awareness can come to us in a glimpse—as, for example, when we have a profound or life-changing dream: a timely message from your mother, long dead, the vision of an angel. Or it can be given to us in silence or meditation, when the chatter of our minds recedes and we enter a void of such grand serenity that the normal hassles and even the valid undertakings of life seem suddenly ridiculous. We may also be encompassed by this radiant awareness in times of great tragedy or profound emotion when we are affected so deeply that the ordinary priorities of life are suddenly shifted, and we see that nothing else matters but love.

The death of Princess Diana was such a moment. In the midst of the quelling of such an exquisite radiance, we are moved beyond our personal fascination with her celebrity to contact the love she embodied with our own love, and to join in that sacred, overarching essence in which we all share. The same is true of Mother Teresa. Her own work was finished, but the love of her labor remains and in her death we are all called into it.

We see at such moments, through our powerful emotions, that we have a palpable connection to these souls we never met, that their work is ours, their love is our love—the one love we all share—and that our joining with them in spirit is larger than life and longer than death.

The Soul's Dream for Us

The soul has a dream for us, and that is to recognize and remember who we are—spiritual beings having a human experience. The soul has always been holding this memory for us, the way a shell holds the sound of the sea and we can hear it if only we hold the shell to our ears. The soul has held this dream for us through all of time, through everything, but now it wants to transform this dream into a beautiful reality. And that is why, instead of just hiding out in the back room as it has been willing to do for aeons, the soul is now making insistent demands in every part of our lives.

That's why, for example, we can no longer live in the world as mindless mongers of its resources. We have done that, but now we see that as a result of our egregiously self-serving relationship to it, the planet has started to respond. Pollution arises, weather goes haywire, strange jungle microbes strike back, creating unmanageable diseases. Stunningly wily microbiotic intelligences are making decisions for us. Their ability to kill us is suddenly, shockingly, far greater than our ability to kill *them*. In beautiful and frightening ways, we see that we are interconnected—with the world, with people, creatures, microbes, weather, the air, the electromagnetic pulse, and even with the machines of the world. We can no longer simply, unilaterally, have our way with things.

This message of our exquisite interconnection is also emerging in our relationships. We're no longer in charge of them; they are directing us. We're not just meandering along some cozy path with them; we're following the paths that they have laid out for us. They're not just "what we do" anymore. They're stunning, demanding, a spiritual workout. They've become so strange and difficult that we can't just pass them off as one of the experiences we're entitled to have simply because we're alive.

Instead of stumbling into them just because they "show up" or even "seem right," we're starting to ask ourselves the larger questions: Why am I really involved with this person? What is becoming of us because of the unique configuration of our connection? What is our purpose here? What's the surprising truth or great lesson that is emerging, the wild rose blooming in the vegetable garden? Through our relationships, our souls are insisting on new, high-level growth, big change. The invitation to a soulful relationship was always present as an option, but now we can no longer avoid acknowledging that our relationships are a work of the soul. Through the challenges within them and the havoc of our relationship lives as a whole, the soul is insisting upon this awakening. It's as if we're being taken on a forced march through a mind-bogglingly complicated obstacle course that ultimately will confront us with our eternal radiance.

This insistence to discovery will be present, whether a given relationship seems "ordinary"—that is, is a conventional marriage—or extraordinary—doesn't conform to the social dictates of daily, domestic, exclusive, or forever. Either way, our relationships are calling us to a world of larger truth and greater love.

We're even directed to this high calling when our relationships end. For example, I know a man, John, married seventeen years, who'd been sensing the oncoming end of his marriage for some time. Although he and his wife, Susan, had never been particularly unhappy, it seemed, as he said, that they had already given each other all they were meant to give, and he felt that for his own growth, he needed to move on.

He wasn't sure if his need was of a spiritual nature, or if it meant having another intimate partner, but he was clear that the time for their parting had come. When he told Susan, she was initially heartbroken, but, as they worked it through in therapy, she, too, realized that in spite of their love for each other, they had gone as far as they could go together. She had supported John in discovering and establishing his career; he had helped her gain a sense of self-esteem. But both of them now seemed stuck in their lives and their relationship was just a holding pattern.

After one of these powerful truth-telling sessions, they went home and made love, and in the tear-streaked aftermath agreed that over the next several months they'd take the necessary steps to effect their separation.

They started to do this, but within seven weeks Susan discovered, to her amazement, that she was pregnant. Having been unable to conceive during all the years of their marriage, she was both delighted and thrown off balance by this discovery. After thinking about it at length and then talking it over, they decided, in spite of their imminent divorce, to go ahead and have the baby and share in their child's financial support and parenting. In spite of this ironic timing, they both agreed that this quite remarkable turn of events in no way changed the fact that *their* marriage was over.

Over the next several months, John and Susan helped each other set up new living arrangements. Meanwhile, throughout her pregnancy, John attended birthing classes with her and together they consulted a lawyer about their forthcoming divorce.

On the day they were to sign the final papers for their divorce, Susan went into labor. Bypassing the lawyer's office, John rushed to the hospital to assist her in the birth. Later that evening they drank champagne in her hospital room, rejoiced in the arrival of their daughter, and signed the papers for their divorce.

As astonishing and untoward as this divorce appeared to be, it held a high purpose for all the people affected by it. Two years later Susan married a divorced man with two sons who moved happily into the role of having a little sister, while John, who'd been a real estate executive, completely revamped his life by totally withdrawing from his professional responsibilities. He took a long time off, hiking and meditating in the mountains, taking instruction in a number of spiritual disciplines. Finally, he went on a series of spiritual pilgrimages. Over time, his focus shifted from his outer to his inner life.

As time went on, their daughter was revealed to be a remarkably unusual child, highly attracted to animals and birds, deeply intuitive. Although her mother and stepfather provided her with family and security, they were unable to support her spiritual emergence, but because he had been on a spiritual journey of his own, John was able to provide her with comfort and direction.

The personality would shudder self-righteously at the audacity of John's leaving Susan at the brink of childbirth. But John's intuition, Susan's trust in his intuition, and their shared courage, created, in the long run, both a nurturing home and extraordinary support for their daughter's developing spiritual consciousness.

We may not know what the soul is up to, and it's often a long way into the story before we can even get a sniff of what it has in mind for us. If we can surrender to the fact that the soul knows what it's doing in spite of travails, confusion, and what at times may even appear to be insanity (as in this man's untimely departure from his wife), we can learn something important from every relationship experience. But, like John and Susan, we must have faith, courage, and integrity every step of the way.

Through their experience these people all expanded their capacity for love. Susan rose to a higher love for John even as they were parting so that, together, they could both rise to a higher level of love for their spiritually gifted child. Susan's new husband was expanded by his appreciation for the gifts that only John could give to his stepdaughter—a set of values missing in his own life—and his sons both opened their hearts to love a remarkable little girl.

Soul-Directed Evolution

The soul is a majestic master. As it takes dominance in our relationships, it is asking for evolution, union, and consciousness. Evolution is continued growth—as individuals and as a species. And not just to make sure that we will survive, but to move us to higher and higher levels in every area of our existence. This means not just breaking through our physical limitations by flying to Mars, breaking Olympic records, or extending our life spans, but also emotional clearing and spiritual expansion.

Union is the sense that we're all in this together, not just as people who are trying to keep the planet from dying off before our grandchildren inherit it, but the awareness that we are all interconnected and, in fact, are all part of the one universal consciousness. Consciousness is all-inclusive awareness, the recognition of the interconnection and the ability to actually experience it at moments or for extended periods of time.

As we move toward this all-inclusive awareness, we begin by being aware that we are self-perceiving beings—that is, we can look at, have feelings about, react to, and in some way know ourselves. We're able to see, for example, that we're plain or beautiful, tall or short, funny or shy, and we can feel good or bad about these observations, respond to them with grace or indignation. Adding all this up—our perceptions and how we feel about them—we get the "gist" of who we are. This is self-awareness.

But as we evolve, this awareness gradually expands and we are also able to see, have feelings about, respond to and "know" other people, creatures, and things. Because of our accurate perceptions of them, we can now respond to them with intelligent, appropriate care. At this level we become capable of empathy, compassion, and nurturing.

At its furthest reaches, our consciousness becomes what is spoken of as "enlightenment," a fully knowing awareness of all people, creatures, and things in all times and worlds. Most of us will not reach this level of awareness, but all of us are on the path that is moving toward it. We are all at a different place on that path. Some of us are still struggling just to get acquainted with ourselves—and we may spend a whole lifetime doing just that. Others, like the little girl in the story, are especially spiritually gifted, and can tune into the connection with other creatures and people through unique gifts of vision or knowledge. Still others, saints, spiritual teachers, and illumined beings like Jesus and Buddha, are in touch with this awareness all the time.

Wherever *you* are on this journey, the soul is using your relationships to help you move further down the path, to a greater awareness of your eternal spiritual being and to a greater capacity for love. You may be being asked to speak the truth, to trust in the goodness in the universe, to find your soul's purpose in being here, to move beyond your prejudice and open your heart to more people. Whatever stands in the way of your capacity to love without reservation will be brought up as a challenge for you to face, embrace, and transcend.

That's because the agendas of the personality are now being asked to defer to those of the soul. We are changing from personality- to soul-driven relationships. What this means is that we are being asked to move from what we want for ourselves—that is, what our personalities want from our relationships—to what the soul, that vastly larger consciousness, wants *from* them *for* us.

As this transformation progresses, we will no longer have relationships that simply serve the function and structures of society through our "wanting to get married," "making a commitment," or "having a family." Nor will we simply be serving our own emotional needs—trying to feel good, having our every want satisfied, healing our wounds. Even people who, on the surface, may appear to be leading charmed lives—the ones who seem to have relationships that include wealth, success, a beautiful house, a fine car, and promising children—are being asked to look at their relationships from a new, enlarged, and challenging vantage point—from the soul level.

I know a gorgeous young couple, William and Christine, who met by chance when he, a Northwest composer, was vacationing in New York, where she, a model, was earning thousands of dollars a week posing for the covers of fashion magazines. Their courtship, romance, and marriage were the epitome of a transcontinental romance. They took an Easter vacation to the Greek islands, where he proposed. They had a magnificent wedding at St. Patrick's Cathedral, and a month-long honeymoon on an African safari, followed by four days of decompression on the Seychelles. Their lifestyle was so luxurious that even all their high-powered glamorous friends were jealous.

A few years into their marriage, they wanted to have children. When Christine had difficulty becoming pregnant, they consulted a fertility expert and a pregnancy resulted. Unfortunately, eight months into the pregnancy, she delivered a stillborn child. After a period of grieving, they went through the fertility process again, and once again Christine became pregnant. All seemed to be well, but after an amniocentesis, it was discovered that she was carrying twins and there was some indication of possible birth defects. The couple was now faced with a difficult choice: they could abort the pregnancy entirely, or Christine could carry it to term, not knowing if the potential birth defects would, in fact, materialize. Having lost their first child, they decided to see the pregnancy through. Because of her age and various complications, Christine was required to spend four months of her pregnancy in bed. During this time, her husband's mother died of a heart attack. Finally, the twins, a boy and a girl, were born, the girl with Down's syndrome, the boy with cerebral palsy.

As William and Christine have gone through the anguish of raising their two infants, I have seen them, time and time again, reach their emotional limits. They say that they have moved from grief to outrage to surrender. Finally, in therapy, they glimpsed the truth that this was some larger lesson, that it was beyond the managing of sleepless nights, feeding schedules, doctor's appointments, and keeping up on the latest medical research to try to effect a miracle. They realized that they are here, above all, to love one another, and that even through the ongoing, taxing, exhausting experience of raising their children, they are here to love these children no matter what. They have been moved, lifted up, transformed.

They also have come to understand that through this process they are a living demonstration to their business associates and friends that this labor of love is of far greater value than all the beauty and accomplishments for which they were each recognized in the past. With one another, in their own relationship, they are now experiencing a love that far transcends the romantic trappings of their past, a love so profoundly grounded in the real, exhausting, and beautiful demands of their present that its power is inescapable. They feel united, not only with one another but with suffering parents and suffering children everywhere. Their relationship has cast them into a larger frame. In the past, they knew the meaning of glamour and success; now they know the meaning of real love.

Although on the surface most of us may still appear to be living simple, "normal" relationships, like this couple we are *all* being called to higher and higher levels of spiritual evolution. Your own experience of this call to consciousness may not be as vivid or grueling as this particular couple's. You may be being asked to forgive your spouse for attributes which seem unforgivable, to have conversations about topics that scare you, or to keep your mouth shut and listen instead of instantly blabbing out all your feelings. Whatever the form of your awakening, your nudge to a higher level, you *are* being called to it now. This is the soul's demand upon us. We are all being forced to reach for more than we can comfortably grasp. And whether or not we choose to be consciously aware of it, all our relationships are asking for this, requiring that we serve something on a soul level.

The Soul Speaks

The soul is insisting that we become ourselves fully. Our souls keep putting our emotional work before us, asking us to complete it so we can start to experience ourselves as the spiritual beings we are.

The soul is relentless. It keeps moving us in the direction of resolving our psychological issues because these are the issues that keep us attached to the personality's concerns and thereby separated from our true spiritual nature, our divinity. The more we face our emotional issues, the less they have a hold on us. The less they have a hold on us, the more we are able to move toward our spiritual awareness. We are here to continually refine and purify ourselves, like a snake casting off its skins—until we are peeled down to our essential spiritual essence.

When it comes to our individual relationships, the soul wants us to heal so that, instead of being stuck in old wounds, we can move to higher ground. Instead of being fixated at the level of betrayal, of childhood pain, or of what's fair, the soul keeps urging us toward love. Instead of staying obsessed with the relationship that "failed" or the person who "failed you" in a particular relationship, the soul invites us to say, "I'm hurt, but I long for resolution. I loved you once and I still hold you in that love. You may have betrayed me, but my soul—my love—is bigger than your betrayal. We went through our ordeals, but there were important lessons. We have been polished, shined, and made new."

The soul always says, "Love is larger than pain; you can still love the person who has wounded you. Return to the love that is your true condition, in which betrayal is an episode and not a destination. You may have been betrayed this time, but next time perhaps you will be the betrayer. Through this you will learn compassion."

Like a wise kindly parent, the soul is willing patiently to teach the personality while it grows into the fullness of spiritual maturity, becoming more and more capable of love. That's because the soul has only one interest, one occupation, one purpose, one pastime, one project, and one eternal destiny—and that is to love. In fact, it will insist upon love, knowing that everything else is fodder. Everything else is just preparation.

The soul comes from a place beyond feeling, and its territory is love. Grounded in the awareness of its own vastness, the soul knows that it encompasses all.

The soul keeps carrying us to love. At the soul level, the pain we feel about all the ruptures in our relationships isn't the pain of injustice or incomplete revenge: *it is the pain of wanting to love and having that impulse cut off, cut short.* It is the pain of having the longing to love with no place to put it, no one to deliver it to, no form, no vehicle for its expression.

The personality draws a small circle, and from within its self-focused circumference, keeps trying to have all its needs met, becoming frustrated and self-righteous when they're not. The soul, however, draws a huge circle that includes everything and everyone, a circle with a circumference so huge that it embraces all opposites. The personality blames, judges, tosses aside, casts out, and plays the victim, while the soul says, "There's a bigger agenda here, a larger frame, an infinitely more complex picture. Stand back and behold it all. See how every one of the pieces fits."

Love's True Magnitude

A couple I know demonstrate the largeness of spirit that can occur when you allow yourself to open to love's true magnitude. Charles and Margaret were married and had six small children. After a number of years, Charles gradually faced the fact that he was gay. He hadn't wanted to believe this, had himself been in denial for years, and felt terrible about telling Margaret, but he finally did. After her initial shock, she realized that at some level she wasn't entirely surprised, and she was moved to compassion. She walked through her own fear and revulsion and told him she was sad for him and also sad for herself.

Instead of being derailed by this crisis, she opened. She asked Charles what he wanted to do, and when he said he wasn't sure, she suggested he go on a journey and if it befell him, to explore having a relationship with a man. She said she didn't want to hear about it unless it was important for him to tell her, and she asked that, in any case, he come home.

Charles did go on a trip. He met many men and he had a heartful sexual relationship with one, a man who lived far away but wanted to make some changes in his life.

Charles came home to Margaret, and because his experience had affected him so deeply, he did tell her about it. He told her that he knew he now needed to have a relationship with a man, and he offered to leave her so she could make a new life of her own. After more discussion, tears, a million questions, a thousand concerns, embarrassments, and fears, Margaret moved through the anguish of the ordeal and the chaos. Finally she asked if there was any way Charles's new lover could move to their town, so that they could continue their relationship. This was her beautiful surrender.

Charles was stunned. Overwhelmed. His heart flooded with admiration, with compassion for Margaret, who, in spite of the strangeness and the pain, continued to stay on the journey with him. Perhaps there was, he told her; he would see. She said she would support whatever developed, but asked that whatever transpired between the two men, Charles would continue to remain visibly and officially her husband and live at home until their children were grown.

Charles agreed to this, and with great love and trepidation, the two of them set out on this extraordinary journey. Charles's lover moved to their town and took an apartment close by. He and Charles continued to have their relationship; Margaret and Charles continued to have their relationship, and the children continued to have a mother and a father who lived together.

Charles, so moved by his wife's expansiveness, began to love her more in a remarkably deep way, the way of the soul. He saw her stature as a soul and he honored her for it. He always spoke of her with the highest admiration, gave her beautiful gifts, and celebrated and honored her in the presence of their children.

In time, the children were introduced to Charles's lover as a friend and, on the continuing but infrequent occasions they saw him, enjoyed him. Meanwhile, Margaret took a lover and had a brief relationship that brought her balance as a woman.

Until his death, Charles continued his relationship with his lover. Margaret and Charles were married forty-nine years, and were always spoken of with the greatest regard. People were always moved by what they perceived to be the spiritual depth of their relationship, a quality of honoring one another rarely seen in a marriage.

We often speak of unconditional love, but how, exactly, we each will be asked to live it out is a challenge beyond our imagining. This couple faced and embraced the unembraceable. They lived in a relationship that contained an unspeakable contradiction, but instead of hiding, denying, pretending, judging, or avoiding, they asked their love to expand, their marriage to stretch, to contain huge opposites.

While on the level of the personality, we might consider their behavior to be denial, bad judgment, or sheer cowardice, on the spiritual level where this couple chose to enact their relationship, it was an expression of love of scintillating proportions. Its true measure was not that they stayed together, that their marriage survived, or even that it continued to "pass" as a marriage in the public eye. Its true grace was the transformation that occurred within the people themselves, and in the radiance they embodied because of having done their spiritual work. They cast off layer after layer of hopes, fantasies, and expectations. Through the agony of their "irresolvable" situation, they were both transformed. In the midst of anguish, they claimed a love more strangely pure than any that could have sprung from letting go of their relationship or from pretending that its terrible complexity did not exist.

The true measure of the soul at work is radiance in the lives of the human beings who have walked the path toward unconditional love. These two people embodied it.

The Tidal Wave of Change

Because the soul is acting in the realm of our relationships, we are now undergoing a tidal wave of relationship reconfigurations; we are being asked, more and more routinely, to do such seemingly impossible things. The soul is saying that the forms of our relationships aren't big enough, if we just keep living them as we have been, to contain the magnitude of love that is now seeking us. We're being pulled, yanked, and cajoled into seeing, to knowing beyond the shadow of a doubt, that love is larger than all the forms we've tried.

The truth is, we are being asked to surrender to the soul's making mayhem in our midst. We don't want to, of course. It's difficult, it's scary. It's making a mountain of chaos out of the molehill we once knew as our relationships.

And in the same way we don't like to think that the earth, the planet we live on, is undergoing some irreversible changes, we don't like to consider that this tempest in the relationship teapot could be taking us on a journey with no return. We'd like to think that whatever strange exception we're living is just that—a weird, strange, momentary exception—and that once all this chaos dies down, we'll be able to mosey quietly back to the way things once were.

For example, I was talking recently with a man, married for sixteen years, who said, with stainless-steel conviction, "I'm committed to my marriage; I absolutely intend to have it last the rest of my life; and I think everyone should renew their commitment to marriage."

He then went on to say that his marriage had gone through a five-year period during which he'd had more than a dozen affairs. He'd nearly lost his wife as a consequence, but the growth they'd gone through during those difficult years had forged a remarkable new relationship. Still, this man didn't want to hear about any tidal wave of change, let alone ride it—although he already had. He said he just wanted to stay married—that was it. Even though his marriage had gone through a profound transformation, he was still terrified of change *as a concept*, and he thought that anyone who could avoid it probably should.

As we continued to talk and he got more specific about what had occurred, it appeared that he had been on a remarkable journey. His affairs had shown him his profound emotional need for the feminine nurturing which his wife, embroiled in the heavy demands of being a high-powered business executive, had been unable to give him. When she discovered his infidelities, she was, understandably, in such overwhelming pain that she attacked him with self-righteous indignation. But then, as they went through it, she with rage, he first with defensiveness and then with his own quite vulnerable revelations, she melted. She reconnected with the feminine in herself, which, long ago, because of the heavy demands of her work and her husband's ensuing neglect, she had gradually abandoned.

Plodding and sifting through the ruins of their marriage, they melted . . . together. They became acquainted . . . for real. Not only did they identify their long-term issues and resolve problems on a personality level, but they recognized that some larger force—the soul—had brought them together for a profound awakening. Only a man who had betrayed her femininity so flagrantly could cause this woman to long for it so much, to fight for it so fiercely, to finally reclaim it.

What they both began to see was that, in spite of all the assaults on their marriage, their deepest relationship was one of unassailable love. At the deepest level—the soul level—they were totally committed to one another.

They also saw, through the lens of their own suffering, that the feminine had been everywhere abandoned to the harsher, more aggressive, more competitive male consciousness. Humbly, without ego, they felt that what they had been through was emblematic of the times. Instead of receptivity, softness, and surrender, the whole world, it suddenly seemed, was being hauled along by effort, competition, domination, an abdication of the heart to the power of the mind. Through their own relationship gone awry, this couple saw a world crying out for the healing of the feminine.

I found it interesting that, in spite of the immense transformation this man and his wife had obviously gone through, at the outset of our conversation he himself was still terrified of change. Although the story he told was one of profound and beautiful transformation, it was almost as if the true meaning—or the larger implications of it—escaped him. His marriage had made its rite of passage; he and his wife had passed through the eye of the needle. But even so, it was difficult for him to imagine that others, too, would have to do this.

What his story teaches is that we can never underestimate how profoundly our personalities are committed to the status quo, how basically entrenched they are, how generally unwilling to change, and how *even when we have gone through changes that bring us to the spiritual level, we may still be in denial.*

And it is *because* this is true that the soul must take such radical measures to make us wake up. Not just a bad day, a couple of arguments, or even a couple of repetitious relationship riddles we can't quite solve. But a vast upheaval in our relationship lives—staggering divorce rates, burgeoning stepfamilies, strange new forms of relationships, ordeals and chaos everywhere. The soul is an ax; it cuts to the quick. It wants us to learn how to love.

That's the reason that, like this man and his wife, so many of us are being taken through so many relationship changes, dragged against our will to where we don't want to go. And like this man, in spite of receiving many actual emotional and spiritual benefits from these demanding transformations, most of us still hope to get our marriages back into the box. That's because, like this man, we're not registering the benefits we're receiving from the changes. We're still resisting the call of the soul by fixating on the old forms of relationships.

In truth, whenever we're given an experience of love and transformation it is the pearl beyond price, ecstatic and, for a moment at least, utterly transforming. But we forget so easily; it's as if we think of these transcendent moments as exceptions to what we're supposed to be doing, instead of as the whole point of our existence.

That's because change in a culture or in an individual life is so profoundly upsetting that even after we've gone through it, we still hope that we can go back to "the way it used to be." As participants in this, by now, clearly unavoidable journey of relationship transformation, we must remember that, as in any journey of evolution, *the changes in our behavior are always ahead of our thinking*. It is through the events we are called upon to live through—divorces, infidelities, serial relationships, sickness, deaths, and a thousand other challenges—and not our reactionary hopes, dreams, memories, or wishes that we will be shown where we are actually meant to be going.

Thus, quite apart from our wishes, our relationships are

creating themselves in wild, new, beautiful, and terribly upsetting forms. They are creating the demanding experiences that are necessary for us to expand as human beings and as spirits. All our relationships are in the process of melting, if not from without—as the form of marriage itself is dissolving—then from within, where we ourselves are melting down. They may still have all the earmarks of traditional marriage, but even inside that familiar framework, spiritual convulsions are occurring, creating epochs of growth we never intended and transformations we never imagined. In these intense and unusual scenarios, as this man's story shows, even infidelity, rather than being the death kneel to a marriage, can become the crucible stage of its spiritual development.

And in the same way that infidelity or any other crisis may initiate the ordeal which ultimately leads to transformation in a marriage, a marriage itself may be only a single step in our life's work of relationships. Instead of being *the* container, it has become *one* of the containers of love. The soul is shifting our relationship focus from form to content, from rigidity to flexibility, from containment to expansiveness, from our emotional needs to real love.

Chapter 6

On the
Sacred Frontier

The Nature of
Soul-Driven
Relationships

The sacred frontier is the wild new relationship fringe
that we are all starting to dance along. The sacred frontier is
soul territory. It's where the soul has stepped in, put its foot
down, and left an imprint on the wet sand of our lives. It is
marked by the extraordinary relationships we are starting to
live and the remarkable relationship exceptions we're trying to
scrub out of the seams of our lives.

As it asks for transformation from the people who inhabit
these unusual relationships, the soul is being both generous
and demanding. It's sending us out on expeditions that, because of their unfamiliarity, are difficult, and delivering us to

new landscapes that are breathtaking in their beauty. The people who either consciously undertake or finally surrender to these relationships are relationship pioneers. They are expanding the boundaries of love.

What this means in real life is that out among the statistics that commemorate our relationship changes are people who are actually loving in new ways, with new attitudes, in new configurations of connection. They may be living in multiple-person relationships, relationships that defy age or gender boundaries, or embody astonishing emotional or spiritual acrobatics. This is already happening, but as time goes on, instead of seeing these relationships as failures or aberrations, people will be voluntarily—even happily—creating these new forms. And eventually, instead of being shocked by these relationships, we will comfortably seek them out.

People who are already living in these configurations are pathfinders; their relationships are exemplary. One way or another, because of a real life experience *in relationship,* these human beings have actually become able to transmit and embody more love. Forging ahead on the sacred frontier of new relationship possibilities, they are clearing the way for us all.

In a way, we're all on the frontier. Sometimes this frontier is a boundary within a relationship we thought we could never cross, a limitation we could never imagine breaking through. We stumble on an infidelity and instead of judging or going berserk, we look for our own part in the betrayal, and rebuild the relationship anew. Instead of constricting, we expand. We go through a tragedy together—a child dies, an illness takes over—and instead of blaming, our hearts are broken wide open. Or life becomes banal and ordinary, and instead of giving up, we take a step in a spiritual direction—develop a meditation practice, give up a suffocating addiction.

Sometimes this frontier is in the kind of relationship we find ourselves creating. It doesn't look right. It doesn't give us the things we expected. It doesn't stand up under social, parental, religious, or even our own scrutiny. It makes us swallow our pride, our egos, our plans, our convictions, our wills, and our personal sense of direction. One way or another, because of what's going on in the relationships we find ourselves falling into, we are being spiritually remodeled.

Your own jaunt on the frontier may see you marrying again and again, living your relationship life among a mottled mélange of friends instead of with one regular partner, or even living alone. You may find yourself falling in love at the most unacceptable moments, or with the "wrong person" of the wrong age, race, sex, or social background. Whether your relationship contains more deviations than the myths allow or fewer goodies than most people would insist on as the necessary contents of a so-called real relationship, you're doing your time on the sacred frontier.

All these relationships point to the future of love—vast love, love beyond boundaries, love beyond conventions and tradition, love without rules and fears, love without preconceptions and judgments, love without outdated myths—*love which can actually be experienced*. And the people who are treading these frontiers are showing all of us that it can be done, that such love is the human future, and that in time we will all partake of it.

What Does the Future Look Like?

The first notion that is being challenged on the sacred frontier is that a marriage is the best relationship form. In the past, what mattered was that the container called marriage, the form, be preserved at all costs. As a result, we incessantly wondered if our marriages could "be saved." We "saved" many marriages which went on to stifle many people, but we were relieved because the form remained intact.

But the soul is interested in content, not in form. It keeps asking the larger questions. "Can this marriage be expanded?" it asks. "Can it be deepened or exalted, can it be truly sanctified, can it be a step on the path to somewhere else?" Interestingly enough, these are the very questions that those on the sacred frontier are also asking, consciously or unconsciously.

In the past not only did we bow before the sacred cow of marriage, we also operated from the perspective that the marriage relationship itself had a validity above the lives of the individuals in it, and that it, as an entity, *must* be saved. The soul doesn't necessarily subscribe to this agenda. It is interested in the individual souls who inhabit this marriage. It asks that a particular relationship serve them, their growth, their development, their illumination. The soul asks for whatever forms of relationship will serve the evolving individual souls within them, not necessarily for the preservation of any particular form. And, from what is already surfacing, with the soul in charge we can conclude that in the future, our relationships will be even more curious and various.

The Medium of Connection

To get a sense of where we are going, we need to look at what I call the medium of connection. Each relationship has this connection, some special way of being together that keeps bringing the people in it back to one another. A medium of connection is that mystical—or very ordinary—thing that forms the crux of a particular relationship bond. It may be obvious, such as both of you always wanting to talk about your feelings, or as esoteric as the two of you building a catalogue of North American songbirds. It may be as understandable as being committed to the rearing of your children, or as unique as sharing a love of Ming Dynasty Chinese art. Whatever it is, the medium of connection is the thing to which, no matter how out of kilter your relationship may become, you can always return to find the true pulse of your unique bond with the person you are loving. It's what singles you out as a pair for a little while or a lifetime.

In the future, it is this medium of connection that will define the structure of our relationships. In other words, the thing that brings us together will show us the shape that our relationships are supposed to take. Instead of having a standardized form (like marriage or living together) into which we try to cram all the possible wild and woolly contents (and outrageous expectations) we can imagine, the form will arise out of content. A relationship will be not only an expression but also an outgrowth of its unique particulars. Just as in a painting the final creation emerges not only from the shape of the canvas but also from the specific palette of colors the artist chooses, so the form of our new relationships will emerge from the unique palette of human experiences that we choose to embody in them.

So the people who have a spiritual bond may be together only when they meditate, or go on a spiritual pilgrimage, just as the couple who wants to have children will choose to marry, even after living together for years, while the two young graduate students who truly want only a lover while they're pursuing their degrees will not assume that they want to get married. We won't have value judgments about these relationships. We will see each one of them as serving a need in a higher process of change.

In the past, we have seen the medium of connection as operating primarily on the personality level. That is, we have seen shared interests—that fascination with Ming Dynasty Chinese art, the desire to have children, or to buy a house, or a strong sexual attraction—as driving the relationship. We have recognized the common ground, that area of overlapping similarities, as being the foundation upon which we have built our relationships. And we have seen that, as a result of the things we held in common, we were able to grow and change within our relationships.

But as our awareness of the soul emerges, we will see that it is actually the soul that is operating in all these "attractions," mediums of connections and shared goals and values. The soul's goal for the future of love is to use our attractions to bring us into precisely the relationships that will provide us with opportunities to expand our awareness and gain more of a sense of unity with others. The soul is using the medium of connection to bring us together to fall in love, and then deliver us to the greater lessons it has in store for us. By understanding this, we can begin to see what our souls are up to and what forms our relationships should naturally be in.

Mystery Is of the Spirit

The truth is that the greatest power in any relationship is not form but mystery, which is not of the concrete world, but of the spirit. Perhaps this is what most captivates us about all of our relationships. The mysterious entices, enthralls us, and although mystery refers to something we cannot know in exact human terms or express precisely in words, we bow before it, because intuitively we sense its power to transform us.

So it will be in the soulful relationships of the future. Instead of emphasizing the fact of our shared circumstances—the roof over our heads, the food on the table, the web site, or the car—we will be talking about the ineffable mysterious power that brought us together. We will be asking why we, in particular, are sharing this life, and in the process we may discover things that have nothing to do with this life—some kind of bond or debt or connection that reaches beyond our material existence. We may sense that we have come together with a high purpose, something immediately obvious or only gradually revealed. It may not be as gigantic as saving the world or the Amazonian rain forests, but whether we decide to marry or to spend only an intimate interlude, the power of the mystery will be present in all our undertakings. Raising lettuce or raising children, our surrender to the mystery will move us, in any relationship experience, from the ordinary to the joyful, from the mundane to the sacred.

I have a friend, a man in his sixties, many times married, who for the past seven years has lived alone, and recently fell in love once again. "This time," he says, "I'm taking it slowly. I'm not going to treat this relationship like a grape-fruit—squeeze out the juice all at once, until nothing is left but the rind." This man had finally matured to a level where he could honor the mystery. In framing "the grapefruit rule of love" he was finally holding out for himself the sacred recognition that patience, surrender to the unfolding of the mystery, are essential to the survival of any intimate relationship. We could all use a lesson in tending the magic, nourishing the mystery that romance embodies, lest we get too "old-slipper-ish" about our intimate relationships, and before they have had a chance to blossom, consign them to daily domestic ruts.

A Soul Connection

I believe that, married or not, we all have a unique soul connection with every person with whom we share our relationship lives, no matter how briefly. Whether or not we have actual memories or visions of what exactly that connection may be, we may find ourselves, as we go about the business of our lovely, loving relationships, talking about the mysterious, seemingly inexplicable connections we do have. This is because our *souls* always feel the deeper connection. So it is that, at certain times, when we meet another person, we just "know" that we have a destiny with them, and are instantly willing to pursue it. Or, for reasons we can't understand, we discover ourselves in a relationship with someone we never imagined we'd care about. At other times, in the midst or at the end of a seemingly ordinary relationship, we are surprised to discover the real nature of that connection.

I have a friend, a man, who had a brief affair with a woman who lived on the opposite side of the country. When it ended they stayed in occasional contact, and once, years later, when he was on a business trip in the city where she lived, he decided to look her up. When she answered the phone, she was emotionally shattered; her husband had died of a heart attack two days before. He canceled his business engagements, rushed to her side, and walked her through every step of the sad arrangements. Obviously, he had been sent to comfort her. Only then, long after it ended, was the real purpose of their romance revealed.

Similarly, when my mother was dying, I decided to stay at a lake resort not far from the town where she lived, so that I could be near her. When I went into the village center to do some shopping one morning, I casually bumped into the same man at three different times. Later that afternoon, when I was sitting in a café writing, the same man appeared once again. "Are you following me?" I finally asked him with a smile.

"No," he said, "but we *do* seem to be in all the same places at the same time."

I invited him to join me, and as we talked, I discovered that he was in the midst of a painful relationship breakup. I had written a book on the subject and happened to have a single copy of it with me. I gave it to him and he gratefully received it. Over the next several weeks, while he was recovering from the trauma of his lost love, he insisted on driving me to and from my mother's hospital bed, a gift I gladly received from him. At the end of my time there, when he delivered me to the airport, we realized that our meeting had been soul-destined, a much needed gift to both of us in a season of shared suffering. We remain friends to this day.

Inexplicable events and pairings are actually the soul at work. The soul is bringing us together with other familiar souls now embodied in the people with whom we are meant to share portions of our lives. Sometimes these attractions may be ancient soul connections renewed. Sometimes they are debts fulfilled or stories completed. Sometimes they are introductions to some further aspects of our soul selves. The time you spend together may be very brief; as if it were only a bow or a curtsy at the end of a play, a momentary recapitulation of some past experience. Or it may be a year-long or even a lifelong marriage with children. Whatever its form, we are all being reborn together, and the more we allow the mysterious force of our souls at work to guide us, the greater the love we will give and receive.

Chapter 7

Illumined Relationships

The New
Forms of Love

As we have seen, it is a movement to greater love that is changing the forms of our relationships, and not, as we have imagined, some failure on our part. The soul is saying that the old forms don't fit, and that through the changing of the *forms* of our relationships themselves, we will be shown the future.

It is precisely because we have been so attached to the forms that they must change. If they didn't, we might think that we're just supposed to get better at what we're already good at—raising families, healing our wounds—and not be able to see that at this point in our psychospiritual evolution, it is Love and not a particular form that we are looking for. This is why, although we have experienced great psychological changes and healing within the traditional forms, we now need new ones. The old forms have done as much as they could to teach us about love. And now the new forms in and of themselves are communicating to us the magnitude of the love that our souls are really seeking.

Frightening as these changes may sound, the transformation of relationships doesn't mean that marriage will die. It means, rather, that marriage will be exalted. I was once at a dinner party where every one of the eight couples at the table had been divorced at least once. Except one. This couple had been married for twenty-four years and everybody asked them, "Why are you still married? What's your secret?"

The husband answered by saying, "We've never had a trivial conversation in twenty-four years." They then went on to explain that very early on, they had each realized that the other had tremendous competence in a number of very specific areas of life conduct, and so they had always deferred to one another in those areas. As a result, they spent very little time dealing with how the usual host of domestic problems would be solved. Whenever they had a conversation, it was always about a book they were reading, a piece of music they had heard, or some deep emotional change that was going on within them. From the outset, they had consciously chosen to conduct their relationship at a very high level.

They also said that their life had been taxed by a major crisis—the prolonged serious illness and eventual death of one of their children—and concomitant highly stressful financial problems. But they had consciously chosen to allow this crisis to bring them to moments of great heights of communication, tenderness, and vulnerability. They spoke of it as "the year they cried together." They said that by the end of it, they no longer felt like a man and a woman, but as if they had melted into two genderless beings who made love in their gender but loved one another as a single soul that had been rejoined. Their experiences, sexually and in watching the gradual, exquisite ebbing of their daughter's life, opened them to their spiritual awareness. From this place they stepped forward into the next epoch of their relationship, not only far more deeply connected than ever before but also with a sacred awareness of all of human life.

From Socks to Prayer

Like this couple, we who choose marriage are all being invited to breathe new life into it, to transform it from a gingham-checked apron to a silken garment of luminous vitality, a sensuous ecstatic wrapping in which vivid, conscious change can occur. We are being invited to make it a sanctified commitment instead of a socially sanctioned habit. Rather than being based on domestic life and habitual patterns—the income, the garbage pail, who made the bed and picked up the socks, child care and the balancing of two careers—illumined marriages will be based on a stunning new depth of awareness. We won't just "settle down"; we will embrace in awe. Our expanded definition of union will be based on a shared consciousness of what is becoming of the two human beings who are cradled in this sacred container. So it is that as married people we will discover a shared spiritual destiny. For those who choose to marry in a conscious form there will be the possibility of elevating marriage—from domesticity to mystery, from the dry cleaners to the altar, from socks to prayer.

It is our willingness to recognize the soul's agenda in every relationship that extends an invitation to marriage, also, to become exalted. Instead of simply replacing marriage with one of the new alternatives, we are being invited to respond to the highest vows it can express, to become one flesh, to cleave profoundly to one another, to consciously go through a journey of transformation as opposed to merely biding our time till death does part us. To the degree that we are able to do this, we are not only rescuing marriage from its recent bad press, but also from the lowest common denominator to which it can dwindle through social and economic demands.

This is not to say that marriage is the path for everyone, or that there is something wrong with you if it isn't your path. But for those who do choose to marry, there is an opportunity to recognize that marriage contains within it an inherent mystery that only our souls can understand, something that requires us to drop our insatiable dependency needs. We are being asked to trust in our souls' deep wisdom, and in the process, we are asking ourselves to expand, to grow upwardly, inwardly, and deeply, to illumine ourselves with fire and light within the boundaries of marriage.

Daring New Forms of Love

As marriage is being reborn, a number of other new distinguishable forms of relationship are also coming into being. That is because marriage, even in its illumined form, can no longer fulfill everyone's needs for intimate relationships. A lot of these new forms already exist and have wormed their way unobtrusively into our midst. It may not seem like they're here because they have been so quietly interjected into the warp and weft of our social cloth, but the mere acknowledgment of them will allow us to see them and perhaps more willingly surrender to their presence.

Marriage Clone

The marriage clone, by my definition, is any relationship which bears all the earmarks of marriage, minus the ceremony or license. (I know a couple who have lived together for twenty-four years who say, "We've had the longest and happiest unmarriage on earth.") There are a multitude of these "unmarriages" already operating in our society now, where two people in love share a roof and responsibilities, including but not necessarily children, some type of economic agreement, a commitment to or some understanding of sexual fidelity, and a postulated future. These marriage clones will continue and increase.

Serial Marriages

We already have serial marriages. We may not have intended them to be so, but they are. The statistic that one out of every two marriages ends in divorce isn't just a phenomenon of first-time marriages. It includes people who marry again—and divorce again—as well as people who have what I call "practice marriages" (a series of short-term live-in relationships), and then settle into the groove of married life with one partner who can go the distance. Others will repeat the marriage process again and again until, either happily or unhappily, they become permanently single.

To one degree or another, most of us will have episodic serial marriages—at least one traditional marriage plus one or several other significant marriages or marriage-clone relationships. This may mean one marriage that "didn't work," followed by another that is satisfying and long-lasting. Or it may mean a series of marriages or marriage-type relationships, each of which demarcates a phase of personal growth or evolution. Whether there is one "failure" followed by a second lifelong success, or a series of "failures" leading finally to one grand or quietly satisfying relationship, serial episodic monogamy will be the most prevalent relationship path of the future. Because of our long lifetimes and the many influences of change that are constantly brought to bear upon us, very few people will have a single lifelong relationship.

One woman, speaking of her relationship preference, said, "I want a lifetime of honeymoons. I love the changes relationships produce. I love the transformations I see in the men I love and my own reconfiguration. It's hell sometimes getting in and out of all these liaisons, but for me, the sorrows and agonies of parting are more than made up for by the ongoing opportunity to fall in love again and to grow in some new direction."

She said that after one short-lived marriage, before she became a successful lawyer, she found that her relationship span was three days (at one of their houses) to three weeks (at a vacation spa, tropical island, or foreign hotel). She was a self-professed lover of romance and felt that, by virtue of having reared three younger siblings after her mother had died, she was unfit for the "long haul of marriage."

I also know a former real estate developer whose four marriages each appeared to represent a dwindling from the one before it. He was married first to the college homecoming queen, the prettiest girl on campus, who gave him two children and a steady but unexciting life. Five years into the marriage, disappointed by the ordinariness of it all, he met a gorgeous woman who awakened his senses and made him feel alive again. He left his wife and ran off with the Barbie doll of his dreams. They were married briefly, ecstatically and treacherously, while he took her skiing at Gstaad, bought the pseudo-Tudor mansion she craved, and lived there with her until the IRS stole the bloom from the rose. When glamour was upstaged by bankruptcy, she left him. He crumbled into the arms of his secretary, who had observed his flagrantly flashy marriage, and hoped that by sheer will she could restore him to his former financial glory. Happy with her attentions, he married her. But when the financial situation remained the same, and they were both disappointed in more categories than either of them could ever have imagined, he eventually left her.

Several years passed and he decided to give up on marriage and his former lifestyle. Not long after he took a position as a postal clerk, a woman stumbled across his path at work. She was a good-natured woman who was neither particularly glamorous nor ambitious. They've been married now for sixteen years. "I've settled down," he says. "I've settled in."

To outside observers, this man's progression of relationships seemed to be a downhill slide as he moved from wealth, glamour, and the homecoming queen to bankruptcy and a simple house in the suburbs. His former friends treat him as if he has failed, but he says that through each succeeding relationship, his fantasies have been peeled away. "I was too impressed with appearances," he says, "my own and everyone else's. I wanted a big life, I wanted to impress people because inside I was insecure. I really had no identity and I was using marriage and the women as a trophy, trying to get a sense of myself.

"The truth is I now feel calm and real for the first time in my life. I've given up all my expectations, my big ideas of what a great life should look like. I never even fell in love with my present wife, but I have grown to love her. And in the process, I've also learned to love myself. Even my relationship with my children has changed. For the first time, I can see them as people and I hope that by watching me they can step into their own lives with better values than the ones I started out with."

This man's journey has been one of coming to terms with himself. Resolving the discrepancy between outside opinion and his own feelings about himself represents a victory of consciousness. He now knows that the less he appears to have, the more he actually possesses. "I lost everything I thought I wanted, and I'm happier than I ever imagined I could be. I finally learned how to love," he says. His soul brought him a great lesson.

The Triangle

In the future there will also be more triangle relationships—committed relationships between three people, which may or may not be sexual. These threesomes can consist of one designated sexually involved couple and a third person, not sexually related to either, who lends support to their union. Or there can be an alliance between three equal friends, whose involvement with each other is such that any one person is being supported by two others.

Consider the couple who share a dear friend, or the divorced remainder of a couple who sustains his friendship with a couple—former friends—after his own marriage has ended. Or, I know three friends, none of them married, whose respective relationships with one another and with their unique union form the core of their relationship lives. Having forged this sacred triangle, they refer at times to each other by the names that most reflect their individual attribute—Energy, Serenity, Dignity. While each of them has other friends and even lovers, they all acknowledge this trinity as their core relationship.

The power of the trinity is unique, often offering outside sustenance when a primary relationship is temporarily ruptured. It also provides balance by taking away the pressure of one person in a couple's having to meet all the other person's needs. But the triangle isn't just about shoring up one couple's relationship, as it might seem. Each person in the triangle has some kind of spiritual destiny with both of the others and is invariably receiving gifts and benefits of equal value.

Among such threesomes, each may well be a member of several threesomes. I know a number of people who claim that this is their ideal form of relationship, and that they move kaleidoscopically among the various threesomes they inhabit, playing a different role in each.

For example, a woman in her late thirties, a computer whiz and part-time masseuse, lives in a household with both her current lover and her former lover. Her former lover, now a good friend, gives her present lover counsel on how to treat her, explaining where he made mistakes, talking about the attributes her current lover has which make *him* more fit for the job of loving her well. He speaks of himself as being the guardian angel to their relationship. "I somehow always understood, even when I was with her," he says, "that I wasn't to be hers forever. I was there to enjoy her and to carry her through a few things, but in actuality, I was just a stop on her way to her real destination."

"We're all having an amazing, beautiful time," says the woman. "It has to be known that two people who love the same person don't have to be enemies. Somebody's got to start living this out and showing how it can work."

In their particular situation, they all support one another in a larger vessel of love. Ordinarily in the world of personality, men compete with one another for the affections of a single woman, not only in the moment of trying to capture her, but even in retrospect. These two gentlemen, both *strong* and *gentle* men, are dissolving the archaic pattern of the male combative mode. In loving this woman together, they also embrace one another as men, which, for each of them, has been a movement toward spiritual expansion.

As their story shows, the soul is always interested in bringing us together. It isn't interested in hierarchies or egos. It keeps saying that love is all that matters. It keeps showing, through each of our little experiences, that if only we can open our hearts just a little bit wider, more love can flow in with every transaction.

Love is ease, love is grace. When we have to worry about such things as "I loved her first," or "I loved her better," or "She left me, so nobody else can have her," we keep constricting ourselves emotionally, physically, spiritually. Constriction takes energy. It wears us out. But each time we can expand, relax, and let more love in, we find a greater sense of ease because we have nothing to defend, protect, or bark about. This is where we're all going, but it takes courage to get there. These people, who are doing it so comfortably, are lighting a candle and showing the way. They have tasted of the true grace which, expanded to infinity, is absolute seamless ease. It is love.

The Double Duo

Another type of relationship will be the Double Duo, as in Bob & Carol & Ted & Alice or even Lucy and Desi and Fred and Ethel. These are two marriages or partnerships which support and complement each other. There's something about being seen from this parallax position that offers grace. When your best friend's husband doesn't know about how vile you become with your PMS, he can continue to honor you as a woman. And when your best friend's sweetheart still thinks you're terrific even though you just lost your job, you can maintain your dignity with your wife. This double duo format provides a profound mirroring of what has grown thin within our own relationships, allowing us to be fertilized and stabilized by another couple, so that within our own relationships we can carry on.

I know two couples who for more than twenty years were, as a foursome, the best of friends. The two women, girlfriends in college, brought their husbands together when they got married, and over the years, the two men also became best friends. As they all grew older, they became uncles and aunts to one another's children, and finally, in retirement, they all moved in together.

For decades, this foursome has been all for one and one for all, and the dramas of fear, loss, joy, celebration, and unequivocal support that they have lived through together have been, for each of them, the crucible of their spiritual development.

Same-Sex Marriage

Same-sex marriages are becoming more and more prevalent, and they are starting to be openly acknowledged by society, that great monolith, always the last dodo bird to catch on to what's already happening. Just around the corner of the future, these relationships will be accorded the social benefits that accrue to heterosexual marriage—the right to marry, to medical care, death benefits, and the usual rights of survivorship.

My friend Josh, after many affairs with men and a long relationship with a lover who died of AIDS, has finally "married" the man of his dreams. Like so many other gay men and women, he and Fred, his partner, wish that theirs could be a relationship legally and socially sanctioned by marriage. At his fiftieth birthday celebration, he drank a toast to Fred as "the husband of my heart."

Cross-Gender Departures

We will also see a blurring of the distinction between heterosexual and homosexual relationships. In our emotional and sexual lives, we *all* possess some of the attributes, attitudes, and predilections of the opposite gender. While we may think of ourselves as "men" or "women," locked into our genders, no matter what our actual biological gender, we also have the feelings, behaviors, skills, inclinations, and passions of the opposite gender. In truth, we are emotional and spiritual hermaphrodites, and there are times when the submerged gender in each of us consciously seeks expression.

Even the most ardently heterosexual women sometimes have a temporary sexual interlude with another woman, while a surprising number of women are actually moving from successful heterosexual marriages to equally successful relationships with women in later life. This same capacity to make a marriage with either gender is also seen among men. Men who claim to have been happily married in every respect may find themselves, at some point, being so sexually and emotionally ignited by a man that they leave their marriages to pursue an interlude—or a lifetime—with another man.

Jane married her college sweetheart at twenty-one, had two children, and after a brief and difficult marriage was divorced by her husband. She then had what she considered to be a very happy marriage with her second husband. But then, at the usual seven-year crisis point in this second marriage, she found herself hopelessly attracted to another woman. She had never before felt such an attraction, felt it impossible to define herself as a "lesbian," and yet she abandoned, as she said, "the only happy marriage I ever had to run off with the woman of my dreams." The two women lived as lovers for three and a half years, but when Jane's daughter got married, she found herself once again longing for the conventions and comforts of heterosexual married life. She rather abruptly concluded her liaison with her female lover and within a year of her daughter's marriage was once again married to a man.

Another woman, the mother of four sons and the wife of a successful corporate CEO, found herself at midlife having one, then another and another affair with a woman. At first she and her husband, to whom she confided her "strange attractions," chalked this up to the influence of the hormonal changes of midlife. But after several years of therapy, she fell profoundly in love with a woman to whom she has now been "married" for nine years. She is happy, now defines herself as a lesbian, and expects this to be the relationship that will last for the rest of her life. When her sons and their children visit her house, they say they are going to visit "their grandmothers."

These excursions—or destinations—with a person of the same gender within or without marriage will become more commonplace. That is, we will acknowledge them more openly. They've always occurred; we've just pretended they haven't. Recognizing that they do won't cause them to occur more often, but will allow us to discover what they mean.

What do they have to teach us? They are telling us about the genderlessness of the soul, showing us that, when we love, it is, in fact, the soul to which we are drawn.

Cross-Generational Matings

A married man in his fifties was an instructor of ballroom dancing. One of his students, a woman about his age, had recently ended a long-standing relationship. Seeing her unhappy one night, he approached her at the end of the class and jokingly asked if she'd like a date with the man that he most admired.

"Who's that?" she asked, intrigued.

"My son," he answered. His thirty-eight-year-old son had recently completed the dragged-out, painful ending of a seven-year relationship and the man arranged for the two of them to meet. They "went out on a date" and have been "dating," as they call it, for three years. They're both too skittish to actually refer to what they're doing as "having a relationship." They tell each other, "I love you," but never discuss the future. Each of them says that the beauty of their relationship is that they live in the continuous present. The woman says he makes her happy, the young man says, "Some things between us are just perfect," and the father says he blesses whatever they're doing.

Although, in the past, relationships between younger women and older men were looked at slightly askance, they have gradually become acceptable. But because of the mystique of a woman's value—or the receding of it being based on her youth and beauty—what still isn't entirely acceptable is a pairing between a significantly older woman and a younger man.

In this story, a man much closer to this woman's age recognized the unique gift that could be shared by his son and his female student. He stepped through the boundaries of his own age prejudice to suggest a relationship that could transform two people he already cared about.

Age is a social as well as a chronological marker. In the past, we subscribed attributes to it that limited the range of our intimate relationships, but in the world of the spirit, there is no chronological age. Beautiful learnings, teachings, and sharings can occur between two people of vastly different ages. This is true in intimate as well as in friendship-type relationships. In fact, there are extraordinary transformations and transmissions, a marvelous generational cross-fertilization, that can occur precisely because two people come from different time frames.

The gradual shift to older woman/younger man relationships is breaking one of the last barriers of prejudice and letting us recognize that in the world of the spirit, we are all ageless.

In this same vein, Arlene, a black woman in her forties who had three grown children, met Jim, a white man, age twenty-two, in a consciousness-raising workshop and, as the saying goes, took up with him. For ten years, they were on again, off again, on again, off again, while they kept saying to each other: this is ridiculous; this is insane; this can't be a relationship; we've got to stop this. Periodically they would get together and have farewell parties, festive meetings where they would have a ceremony, split up, and go back to their "real lives." But every time they did, one way or another, after a while, they'd get back together again. Finally, on the tenth anniversary of their getting together in the first place, they decided that maybe this thing they had was actually a relationship and they should just relax and enjoy it. The woman is now fifty-two, the man is now thirty-four, and they're still together. After years of fighting it, they've surrendered to the fact that this is love.

This couple built a relationship against all odds, and against their own and everyone else's prejudice. No matter how hard they tried to dismantle it, like taffy it just kept sticking to them. No matter what external prejudices we live with—racial, gender, age, or judgments against our size and shape— it's always astonishing to discover the prejudices that reside within us, the relentless inner demand for perfection that we keep imposing on ourselves.

This couple's soul work *was* having this relationship. Against their will, they kept stepping through every single outer and inner restriction, point of view, and social expectation that kept saying, "This can't be love." On the personality level, they were willing to let go of this relationship—it didn't look right and it didn't follow any number of conventional blueprints. But the soul kept urging them across new boundaries, egging them on to love.

They are now immensely happy with one another, and even their personalities are delighted. But the larger measure of their relationship is that they now stand comfortably in the midst of all the differences that they inhabit. Their relationship is a living embodiment of the truth that when the soul steps in, there are no boundaries to love.

The Parent-Child Bond

Recently I had an opportunity to observe yet another unique variation on relationships. While my sweetheart and I were taking a trip up the coast, our car broke down on a remote seaside road. As it conked to a halt and we wondered who might show up to rescue us, a beat-up antique camper sidled up beside us and a man and a woman got out. While the two men discussed the car's ailments and possible cures, I had a chat with the woman. She was an older, salt-of-the-earth, leather-skinned type who swam every day and had been a vegetarian for twenty years.

As I was wondering about the status of her relationship to our passing hero—wife, sister, or cohort—she interrupted our conversation to feed the pair of cats that were mewing inside the back of their van. The big handsome one, she announced, was a boy, and the other, more elegantly feline, was his mother. She then went on to say that she and her son (she nodded toward our rescuer) had been roaming around together camping for weeks at a time here and there for the past seven years. It was obvious that, for whatever reasons, this was their relationship of choice. A variation on the theme of the aging son who won't leave home and spends life with his mother, these people had obviously created a lifestyle of pleasure, vitality, and quiet public service.

A close relationship between a mother and a grown son has been viewed in the past as off-color, but many parents and children will end up having one another as their primary relationship, if not for a lifetime, then for a significant period. Many divorced women and men have consciously or unwittingly chosen their children to be their primary relationship, while single women have also elected to bear and parent children on their own.

Friendship

Friendship is emotional kinship. As one's family is kin in blood, one's friends are kin in spirit. In friendship we entertain the sentiments of esteem and affection for one another, the joy in shared interests that draw us again and again into one another's company, to share the ever-changing vicissitudes of life.

In the past, friendships were often used as rain checks on a so-called real relationship, something we could make do with in the fallow periods between romances. But true friendship is a relationship of great magnitude. It is sacred communion. It is a steady, accurate reflection of self, a balm in time of need, a relationship whose character, precisely because of the lack of sexual involvement, ignites primal and nurturing bonds. In these relationships, in the absence of the emotional challenges that are constantly presented by our sexually intimate relationships, we are nourished, supported, mirrored, and made new. We are cared for.

Friendship relationships are often the sweet revisitation of some ancient soul connections. We relive the memory of being sisters, brothers, parents, or children, members of a tribe or kingdom. These soulful recapitulations of our spiritual connections with one another are among the most exquisite in the panoply of human relationships. But sometimes friendship is consciously chosen as the form for a primary relationship.

Jack, a man in his fifties, and Sandra, a woman in her late thirties, stumbled into the outskirts of an intimate relationship with one another. In his twenties, Jack had been married for six months, and had had, as he put it, "probably a hundred seriously unsuccessful relationships" in the many years following. Sandra had also had a number of brief relationships, and in all of them, both she and her partners had become highly abusive.

As Jack and Sandra began to get acquainted and started telling each other the stories of their respective childhoods, it became apparent that both of them had been profoundly abused. As a teenager, Jack had pimped for his mother, a prostitute. Sandra had been repeatedly raped by her father and a brother. These abuses had been reflected and reenacted in all of their intimate relationships. One night, when they were talking about their histories, they looked at each other and said, "If we become lovers, all we'll do is destroy what we already have." And so, before they had crossed the sexual boundary or further fanned their dreams of romance, they consciously chose to remain just as friends. This is their form of "relationship," and neither of them has another. They have enacted their friendship now for a number of years, and in this humble cocoon, each of them has been able to grow.

In their case, discretion was the better part of valor. They are both in therapy and consciously chipping away at the hyperreactiveness created by their histories of abuse. Having one another as a mirror is helping both of them with their healing. Nevertheless, they each acknowledge that, because of the magnitude of their abuse, they may never actually be able to participate fully in an intimate relationship.

Since love is big and grand and powerful, we'd like to believe that it can solve all our problems, that falling in love per se can make all the demons go away. Both Jack and Sandra had a profound need for love, a desperate void of longing that needed to be filled, and yet, wisely, because of their own limitations, they decided not to pursue it in the usual form.

We need to remember that the soul doesn't always grant our wishes or even respond to what appear to be our obvious needs. It keeps leading us gently to the further reaches of ourselves. These people found love, like a cotton bandage, in the careful friendship they formed. Through being able to see each other as exquisite in spite of their unsavory histories, their circle of compassion was expanded—to include themselves. The soul wants us to love and care for others, but it also wants us to awaken to the suffering and beauty in ourselves. Because of the ugliness of their early violations and subsequent relationship experiences, both of these people thought of themselves as hopeless and unworthy. The soul graced them with the mirror of one another, and gradually, over time, has allowed them to claim the beauty in themselves.

Even apart from such special circumstances as these two people's, friendships are the breath and stuff of many a relationship life. Whether you have been mortally, emotionally wounded or just come to a season in your life where friendship is your highest relationship form, true friendship is always a gift of the spirit.

The Sacred Circle of Friends

There will also be a form of communal relationship that I call the Wheel or the Sacred Circle of Friends. In this configuration, rather than having a single spouse, domestic partner, or main squeeze, an individual will have a collection of loved ones and friends who comprise his or her relationship life. In these formats, each person will be the hub of his own wheel, surrounded by a number of people, each of whom serves a specific relationship function—the confided-in friend, the person who shares in the rearing of children, the person who shares some financial burden, the occasional or serial lover, or the practical helpmate. Instead of this group being viewed as a stand-in for a "real relationship," this constellation of people will be celebrated as a bounteous gift, acknowledged as a relationship form in itself.

Vincent, a man in his forties, is a person whose entire relationship life has been happily lived in this form. Although he has an occasional lover, this wheel is his relationship of record. He is never without company or stimulation but, as he himself admits, his phone bills are enormous.

The Emotional Spouse

A frequent new form of relationship is one in which two people of the same or opposite gender choose one another to be their emotional spouse. An emotional spouse is a person with whom you share all your deep emotional intimacies but with whom, for one reason or another, you choose not to be sexual.

This may be because one or another partner in this relationship is gay, is married to someone else, is geographically unavailable, or shares none of the other aspects—daily life, or a shared household, for example—of a conventional relationship with you.

I know a woman who for more than seven years has been emotionally "married" to a gay man who lives hundreds of miles away. Another has her primary bond with a heterosexual man who also lives far away. In both of these emotional pairings, the relationships are almost daily, are conducted primarily by phone, and are shored up with occasional supplementary personal visits.

These emotional pairings don't necessarily preclude other, sexual relationships. A forty-three-year-old woman I know is legally married to and shares a house with a gay man, whose companionship she enjoys and with whom her domestic life is a daily pleasure. Meanwhile, she has a passionate "intimate" relationship with a man who is her lover and soul mate. They see one another a couple of times a week and most weekends. Why don't they get married? She couldn't stand to live with him.

Breaking the domestic myth, as this woman has, is one of the most difficult relationship conventions to challenge. It is remarkably entrenched. She says, in fact, that people's reaction to her *living with* a gay man verges on the hysterical. "If I were just having the relationship with my lover and living by myself, everybody would be fine with it. But there's something about this who-you-live-with thing that just wigs people out."

This woman doesn't think of herself as a pioneer particularly, but she gets all the flak as if she were a mad scientist. Holding her ground about *both* of her relationships is her act of courage. Her relationship life gives everybody around her a chance to drop one or a dozen relationship prejudices, and in so doing, to learn a little bit more about real love. This is her soul work.

Social Pairings

Along with strictly emotional pairings, we will see relationships that exist specifically for social purposes. Kim is an extremely successful corporate executive whose position in the corporate world is more highly respected if she has a man at her side. So for seven years she has conducted a visible public relationship with Mark, a closeted gay man. A corporate executive himself, Mark's own professional status benefits from their alliance. It allows him to be imagined as her soon-to-be husband and her at-the-moment handsome escort. It protects him from the agonizing scrutiny and judgment that, in his profession, would be brought to bear on him. Her partner at social and public events, he is charming, gracious, and remarkably supportive of her success and successful enough in his own right not to be visibly challenged by her. Their respective colleagues and business partners continue to look forward to their ever imminently forthcoming marriage which never seems to quite manage to occur.

Kim, who grew up in poverty and was repeatedly sexually molested as a child, doesn't really have much interest in having a sexual relationship with a man. She straightforwardly acknowledges that she is not a lesbian and she doesn't hate men. She says, rather, that she's married to her work, that her career is what gives her the most satisfaction, that it's her form of service to the world, and that, unlike many women, she is not really interested in a full-spectrum relationship—meaning one that includes sex.

She's grateful for Mark's presence in her life and enjoys his company. She appreciates that he is willing to serve this decorative social function and admits that his presence in this form is actually what amounts to love for her. "I'm in the odd position," she says, "of actually feeling more loved when I'm not sexually involved with a man. I can't tell you how grateful I am that he's here. I feel protected for the first time in my life." Mark is also relieved to be her social counterpart. Just as he's providing an umbrella of social acceptability for her, she is doing the same for him.

Tradition says that an intimate relationship is sexual—that sexual involvement per se is what indicates that people are in a "relationship." This couple—for they are "a couple" to the world—are graciously, consciously carrying one another through the thickets of social judgment that could prevent them from leading their lives and giving their service as they do. Their "relationship" honors them both. They conduct it with pleasure and gratitude. They conduct it with love.

Voluntary Separations

Lisa, a woman with two children and happily married for six years, has just encouraged her husband, Tim, to accept a year-and-a-half-long assignment in a city four hours away. With the help of babysitters and after-school care, she'll keep her own job as well as being the primary caretaker for the children until the year and a half is over. "It's a stretch," she says.

They both anticipate the resentments that may occur with Lisa doing the major part of the child rearing, while Tim comes home like a guest on the weekends. But they view the situation as an opportunity to reveal some deeper emotional parts of themselves to each other. "We've been emotional wimps in the past," says Lisa. "Our marriage has been lucky; everything has always just sort of smoothly sailed along. It's only since we've been discussing this new possibility that some things we never knew about each other have finally emerged. We're getting acquainted. We're getting real."

It is most interesting that they have *chosen* to undertake this separation, which isn't strictly a financial necessity, but rather a conscious growth experience. Tim had a "good enough" job for years, one that provided well for his family, but his creativity had been suffering. He was feeling the usual male mid-life malaise and, instead of insisting on keeping him trapped in his role, when this unique job opportunity appeared, Lisa, remarkably, encouraged him.

"It wasn't all magnanimity," she says. "It was also my awareness that a man who sacrifices his creativity at work may end up expressing it sexually with another woman, and of course I didn't want that to happen. But we haven't acted out of fear. We both saw this as an opportunity. The deeper truth is that I love him and I want him to feel fulfilled. He's sacrificed for us all these years; it's time for us to sacrifice for him. Best of all, just contemplating this change has already changed our relationship. We're talking about things we never dared to talk about before. And in helping him get situated for the year he'll be gone, we've already had three "honeymoons" in his new bachelor apartment, and the times we're all together as a family have allowed the children to appreciate their father in a way they never did before."

In the past, separations in marriage were considered acceptable only if they were a consequence of brute necessity. A man could go off to sea or to war, or he could be on a scouting mission staking out some new territory to which his family would soon follow. But other than that, separation from one's spouse was tantamount to divorce. Today, in general, separation from one's beloved is still seen as acceptable only during the courtship phase of a relationship.

The soul asks for the experiences that invite the individuals within a relationship to grow. Lisa and Tim see this somewhat cumbersome arrangement as an opportunity to deepen their love by opening the doors to a quality of giving and loving that their conventional marriage never before contained.

The Solo

The solo is yet another emerging form of relationship—a commitment to self in order to be available to other callings of love. In fact, one sixth of the marriageable-age American population is single, and many of them, for a number of different reasons, are *choosing* to live alone. In the "olden days," you were thought to be a misfit if for any reason you chose not to "fall in love," get married, or at least have an intimate relationship that was recognizable as such. Even though women aren't called old maids anymore and men aren't always looked upon with the suspicion of being homosexuals if they aren't married, to a great degree we still expect ourselves and everybody else to be in or to be actively seeking some kind of relationship.

Some people have chosen the temporary single life due to circumstances, such as being occupied in a compelling project like writing a book or getting a graduate degree. Others have had enough of the relationship roller coaster and have in effect put up a billboard saying, "NO MORE!" They may simply be exhausted and have given up, or they are temporarily or permanently choosing a life of deeper reflection. Others choose the individual life so that, as circumstances require, their love can be shared by many—a sick father, a foster grandchild, or a household of stray animals.

A solo is a song sung by a single person, yet it can touch the hearts of many. It calls out from an exalted place and invites those who listen to respond to its all-embracing melody. There's an old woman, Mary, who lives at the end of my street. She's seventy-five years old and still has eyes as blue as the blue on any Dutch delft plate. She was beautiful, you can tell. As she herself said to me one day, "I had many a man look over toward me in my day, but I enjoyed my career, and I was the only girl who had one in those days." She went on to say that twenty years ago she and her sister were hurt in a serious car accident.

She leans on her aluminum cane in the lane waiting for her dog, Lady, to amble up the hill and finally catch up with her. "Then my sister got killed in another car accident and I inherited her daughter, a struggling young widow and *her* two teenage sons. They're all down here with me," she says, pointing her cane in the direction of her house. "I guess I'm still here just to love them," she says, bowed over sideways on her cane, "to help them get all grown up, to see them both through college. And when they've been loved enough, the good Lord will take me home."

This woman has had no intimate relationship at all in her life—in order to be available for the supportive relationships that were to be her destiny. Somehow, intuitively we might say, on a spiritual level she understands that her life's work was to make her home, her financial resources, and her love available to this struggling young family. It isn't very romantic. It hasn't been much fun. At times, the boys drive her crazy, but you can see in her eyes when she talks about them how very much she loves them. In this life, Mary passed on romance and was granted many other things: beauty, a happy career, and a quietly heroic life's work of love at the end.

The Relationship Monk

A number of people have consciously chosen to be single because their life has a higher purpose which requires their solitariness. There wasn't a Mrs. Jesus. That is, Jesus didn't have time for a so-called relationship. Neither was there a Mr. Florence Nightingale or a Mr. Joan of Arc. Some life works are so immense in the demands they make upon an individual that it would be inappropriate at least and wrong at most to subject an intimate relationship to the demands of this other commitment, and vice versa. This is why, in the past, we have had unmarried monks and nuns and gurus.

Sometimes, a series of marriages or marriage-clone relationships or simply the passage of decades results in a personal awakening that causes men or women fiercely to choose life on their own for deeper inner inquiry or for some larger service. In fact, in certain spiritual traditions, when the season of family and child rearing is over, a couple departs from one another and their marriage and moves out into the world to offer the remainder of their lives in sacred service. It is such a tradition, consciously recognized or intuitively acknowledged, that more and more people are choosing to follow.

Intentional Community

As we watch the traditional boundaries of our relationships dissolving, being transformed in one way or another, we are all being moved along in the direction that tells us we can and we must relax our boundaries. All these relationship breakdowns, dissolutions, and transformations are moving us toward community, a state of relatedness in which specific partnership is irrelevant. Community is an amalgam—a melting pot in which the characteristics of all create the coloration and vibration of the single entity.

I know a marvelous woman whose almost entire life of relationship has been lived out in community. Years ago Suzanne was married and had three children. As they were growing up, she divorced, and when they left home, she decided to dedicate her life to the service of people's awakening to their spiritual selves. She remodeled her home and created a number of living spaces for people who shared this goal. With their assistance, she opened her home on a monthly basis to writers, teachers, healers, and other individuals interested in having a spiritual dialogue. As their common awareness developed, they each went back into their own communities and neighborhoods, sharing new ideas on health, relationship, and the environment as avenues of spiritual communion.

Over the years Suzanne's community has continued. Participants come and go as their own lives permit, but a core group forms a steadfast spiritual family. From time to time Suzanne will have a romantic interlude; at other times she laments that she has none. But all the while her priority has been clear. In this gathering, this community, she has been emotionally nourished, and through the leaders, teachers, and healers she has brought together to share their teachings with others, she has also, profoundly, served.

Community is a large container. It is the gathering in of many individuals whose boundaries have relaxed into a blending. It can contain a multitude of variables and hold them all in honor, with the communal consciousness affirming the appropriateness of them all. In contrast to the selectivity and exclusivity of marriage, community includes and embraces. It takes in. This doesn't mean that a particular community—a communal household, for example, or a community gathered to offer service or for its own evolution—won't have its own unique values or make demands upon its members as lovers or marriage partners do. What it does mean is that these values and objectives, instead of arising out of personal needs, will arise out of shared wholeness.

New Forms of the Family

As the future of relationships is approaching us, it is not only marriages but also families that are falling apart and reconstructing themselves right in front of our eyes. The breakdown of the nuclear family has already happened. A thousand social changes have occurred, exposing children, parents, and people in general to a whole new set of relationships.

This breakdown of the family is showing us how sacred family is, and how desperately every child needs two parents. But it is also showing us that the relationships that emerge when families collapse and re-form also have value. They also nourish and expand us. Stepparents, stepsiblings, ex-wives, and ex-lovers can all play important roles in developing our spiritual consciousness. They, too, bring all the gifts and lessons of relationship. We go through all the stations of the cross with them. With them we also grow, transform, and expand our capacity to love.

Our enforced participation in all these reconfigurations can inform our spirits with a precious value and strange beauty all their own. We don't particularly like getting to know all these extra people, growing up with them, being their step- or ex-"whatevers," but we are expanding because of it. These sandpaperish initiations are requiring us to smooth over our rough edges and give true love a whirl.

It's all very complicated and exhausting. We'd like to go back to the way it used to be. As all this upheaval has taken its toll, we have perhaps lamented, resented, and resisted the breakdown of the so-called nuclear family most of all, as if it were the only container for parental and filial love. But as anybody who's lived in an intact nuclear family knows, it can, itself, with its own unique pathology and unrelenting focus, be a kind of living private hell.

Although we'd like to believe otherwise, there's no guarantee that just because it remains intact, a family will be a wellspring of nurturing. Just as marriage qua marriage isn't perfect, families aren't either. If they were, we wouldn't be living in a psychiatric culture. The wounds created by nuclear families are immense; they have broken our hearts and our spirits and put our souls out in the streets. And not—as everybody simplistically assumes—because there are divorces in them (because in many of the worst there was no divorce). But because they are comprised, in far too many instances, of human beings who have excised their true spiritual dimension and consequently don't know how to love.

When it comes to love, the form of the family doesn't matter. The soul is asking us to love, whatever the recipe looks like, whoever the family is.

Even as we are lamenting the loss of the family as we have known it, in the brave new world of relationships a new version of family is emerging—a form of family that invites us to a greater love. Our seemingly catastrophic circumstances are delivering us to surprising forms where the family that holds us is a bigger human community than just mother, father, sisters, brothers. In this new world where children can have four parents and a raft of stepsiblings, we have, in effect, gone back to the tribal family of old, where children grew up with aunts, grandmothers, grandfathers, neighbors.

Although the exact players are different in the sprawling

new configurations, we are once again being called to seek love, to offer it and to receive it. In exchange for the loss of the intense focus and neurosis of the nuclear family, we are receiving the possibility of far greater love. In a sense, the whole human village has become a family.

The Common Thread

No relationship is without its difficulties. The difference between the difficulties in these illumined relationships and those of traditional relationships is awareness, consciousness. In illumined relationships, no matter how odd or seemingly unbearable the challenge, people open, expand, transform. They do this on a spiritual level. They don't simply become better in the psychological arena; they are moved by the larger consciousness within them, the divine soul presence, to open their hearts, to expand to an ever more embracing love.

Our hearts contain chambers that we are not aware of until suffering pries them open. We suffer, and in the process, what seemed unbearable stretches us, breaks us through to a stunning heretofore unimaginable level of awareness.

The soul isn't here to indulge us; it is here to make us reach for the stars. The people in this chapter were all faced with relationships which, in their deviation from the traditional forms, represented a spiritual opportunity: to become bitter and vindictive because their lives weren't matching the picture of a fairy-tale romance or to open their hearts to the gifts that *were* being offered; to whine about their shattered expectations or to rise to the occasion with great love.

These are only a handful of examples, a sampling from all the new and unusual configurations that will occur. Like these spiritual pioneers, you, too, are being invited to push the boundaries of love. Which stretch of the sacred frontier are you on?

Chapter 8

When the
Soul Enters

*The Ten Qualities of a
Soulful Relationship*

As we move consciously toward soulful relationships, a
number of urgent questions emerge. If the soul is in charge,
what will be the defining attributes of a relationship? How will
we know if a relationship is a "good" one, if it is nourishing,
correct, or valuable in our ongoing lives? How will we know
if a given relationship is truly serving our soul's path or our
personality's development, that it isn't just a detour we would
be better off avoiding?

The answers to these questions are to be found in the attributes inherent in all these new forms of relationships. Rather
than outward form, it is these beautiful qualities themselves

that will create the foundation upon which we can build finer, more elegant unions, or if need be, to conduct their conscious and gracious completions.

When we engage in a relationship at the soul level we are submerged, lusciously bathed in the qualities that continually transform it. It's not that we don't have problems, but we approach them differently. Every psychological issue is also a spiritual teaching in opening our hearts, for how we deal with the issue emotionally is always a step toward our spiritual selves. Indeed, our willingness to deal with each issue becomes a journey through which the spiritual teaching is gradually revealed to us.

Although we may go through the seven traditional stages of a relationship, we will trust that each episode has meaning. We will look for the meaning and surrender to what we need to learn, knowing that the soul keeps quietly, steadily bringing us to a higher context, inviting us to open our hearts, to act from love instead of need, and to remember our eternal connection. Consciousness demands that we move through the thickets of conflict and misunderstanding with honesty, generosity, empathy, and compassion. Instead of going endlessly round and round on our personality issues, we can actually resolve them.

We may still wound one another, but when we are functioning at the soul level, we rise to the occasion with forgiveness. Instead of approaching one another from across the abyss of our differences with fear, anger, and self-righteousness, we keep moving toward one another until we arrive together in the middle, aware of our similarities, merged in our blessed union. In this way, the limitations of a relationship are gradually dusted off and set aside, and we ascend in an ever-expanding upward spiral toward greater and greater capacities for love. Through the beauty of our consciousness, the soul engages us in a deeper level of communion with our beloved. This is the soul's inheritance for us.

But, in order to live at this level, we must develop the ten qualities of soul that can actually bring this transformation into our relationships, no matter what their form. To the degree that we cultivate these attributes, and only to this degree, we will be delivered to the genuine love that is our future. That is because these attributes in themselves are the embodiment of love; they are the light, the beacons to follow.

Self-Awareness

Love is a work of the soul, but for it to be so, we must first do the work of the personality and this requires self-awareness. Self-awareness is knowing yourself wisely, truly, and deeply, and acting on that knowledge. Our new relationships are calling us out of the passive patterns of our past to become vividly conscious. This means that instead of stumbling onto the real issues or the real meaning of our relationships after they are over, we are being invited to be aware of them as each relationship unfolds.

This also encourages us to take responsibility for our own lives by being more conscious in choosing our relationships. Instead of just casually presenting ourselves to whoever comes along for whatever relationship seems to appear, willy-nilly, out of nowhere, we must become aware that each moment of our lives is precious and each transformation we share with another person is an unrepeatable breath of our lifetime. The soul is asking us to be active: to think, to decide, and to act consciously in creating each of our relationships, not just to "fall in love," but to *choose* to love. Our frittering days are over; we need to be ruthlessly honest and stunningly clear—with ourselves and with one another. We must choose to have a *real* part-time affair, a *real* marriage, a *real* homosexual partnership, a *real* one-night episode of passion, or a *real* lifelong romance.

Begin by having the courage to ask yourself some real questions: What is the most important thing that you are seeking in a mate? What is it you long to receive and what are you actually willing to *give* in a relationship? Continue, by making self-awareness a priority in every moment in your relationship: How are you feeling now? and now? and now? What is important to you? What teachings are being revealed? How are you learning to love?

Aliveness

Aliveness is energy. It's the juice, the vitality, and the passion that wakes up our cells every morning. It's what makes us want to dance. It is the energy that moves a relationship from the status quo to something grander and much more expansive, something that makes our hearts beat faster, our minds, and our eyes open wider than ever before. Everything is of interest to a person who's truly alive, whether it's a challenge, a loving moment, a bucket of grief, or a glimpse of beauty.

As long as we live, it is our aliveness that creates growth, change, mirth, and possibility. Aliveness is life itself. And so if the relationship you're in now or the one you're contemplating for the future doesn't have aliveness—room for you to feel vivid, wild, exquisitely serene, beautiful, thoughtful, passionate, open, daring, sensual, and sensitive—then perhaps you should look further. In order to be worthy of your soul, a relationship should give you the sense that both you and it are alive—and being continually born anew.

Aliveness *in a relationship* is the sense that something's happening here, that growth is occurring, that, together, the two of you are headed somewhere. When a relationship has aliveness, everything in it will bring you closer to one another, allow you to know each other better, to feel more connected as time goes on.

Relationships conducted at the soul level are always about living. They are about growth, green leaves, change, and transformation. In fact, they are a wellspring of aliveness because when you listen to the directives of your soul, you always grow. You feel vitality, change, and excitement in all your outer circumstances and change in your inner being as well. And as any relationship continues, it is its aliveness above all that keeps us interested in the journey. There's never a dull moment, and as you move from frontier to frontier—although at times you may feel scared about where you're going—you will have a sense of the endless and beautiful unfolding of your lives.

So if you're wondering if a particular relationship really belongs in your group of intimate connections, first, pinch it to see if it's really alive. Do you feel renewed because of it? Do the discoveries and changes you make as it continues to unfold excite you and delight you? Ask where its true vitality lies—in its sexual passion? in your shared love of language? of nature or the ocean?—and then go with what's good in it. From this goodness you will be able to create a relationship that will always be a tribute to its excellence. It will be brilliant and beautiful. It will be strong. It will be an expression of the highest common denominator of aliveness that together you and your beloved can embody, a vivid, living example of what magnificence in a relationship is all about.

Realism

Realism is telling yourself the truth about what is possible in your life. It is personal authenticity, behaving like the genuine article that you are, showing your unvarnished self in all your transactions. It's also the way we look at and discern our mutual realities. That is, it's not just about how *I* feel; it's about how you feel also. Realism is looking at the larger picture that contains more players.

Vastly different from romanticism, realism knows that truth is beauty, and that the only way to be satisfied is to stop deceiving ourselves. But we've all been lying and cheating and fooling ourselves for so long about what we really want out of our relationships that we have no idea how magnificently they might expand if only we could become realistic about them. Instead of creating myths, illusions, fantasies, and impossible expectations (and all the attendant disappointments and breakups), we could create exactly the relationships that work for us. Realism looks at what you actually want, combined with what is actually possible, and then makes decisions based on the working-out of those truths.

In the old romantic paradigms, all we really wanted was to get our needs met, no matter how unrealistic that may have been and no matter how that affected another person. It was all about instant gratification, focusing on what we wanted to happen instead of what was actually occurring. But in our new relationships, instead of being blindly self-serving, we are being invited to consciously create relationships that serve ourselves *and* others and that also hold the potential of bringing us to a higher place. If we can be realistic—which means being both flexible and discerning—we will be able to create relationships that actually *do* provide us with exactly what we want. They will also, not surprisingly, provide the same for the people we choose to love.

I have a client, the middle-aged father of a four-year-old, who after his recent divorce realized that his primary relationship would be with his young son. As a child, he himself had been alternately beaten and abandoned by his alcoholic father. He had never been fathered enough, a profound loss which had created many repercussions in his adult life. He cared deeply for his son and was determined to give him a different experience.

Over several months, he dated two women, both of whom he liked very much. But when it came time to choose, he chose the one who enjoyed spending time with him *and* his son. He explained this to the other woman, who was very disappointed, but eventually she understood. She blessed his union with the woman of his choice, and in time went on to marry a man who, like herself, didn't want children. Although being realistic was painful in the moment, in the long run it benefited everyone.

I also know a woman who, for years, as she watched all her friends getting married, kept saying to herself, "So what's the matter with me? When am I ever going to get married?" Finally, when her best friend walked down the aisle, she panicked, certain she would be an "old maid" for the rest of her life. But as she watched her friend going through all the difficult adjustments of marriage, she gradually began to acknowledge that, in fact, she didn't really *want* to get married. She'd been engaged briefly many years before, and even her engagement had made her feel stifled. She'd broken it off and developed a career, which for her was much more satisfying than having a husband. What she really wanted, she discovered, was to live alone and have a part-time lover and friend.

When she finally admitted this to herself, she put a personals ad in the paper, asking for *exactly* what she wanted. Several men responded, and one of them eventually became her sexual companion. He has lived, at different times, two blocks, half an hour, and two cities away, and together they have enjoyed this unique relationship for eighteen years.

So be truthful about what you're seeking, even if it doesn't look like your romantic dreams or you're afraid of how bizarre it may appear to be. Realism is sacredness in soul-driven relationships because it allows us to create relationships of crystal clarity instead of clouded fantasy. So if it's a sexual partnership you want, go for it. If it's serial, episodic monogamy, accept it. If you want to be a mistress, be one with impunity. If an illumined marriage is your ideal, hold up the banner and live your conscious marriage with the kind of power and beauty that will show the world what a glorious marriage can look like. The point is, create your relationship with candid—realistic—awareness. Only then will you have a chance to get what you really want and to be truly happy. Your reward will be a lifetime of conscious, vivid relationships. One—or hundreds. And in all of them, you will feel loved.

Honesty

Honesty is choosing to live in the truth, and in a relationship that means living moment to moment in genuine straightforwardness. In a soul-driven relationship, the commitment to truth will be paramount. This means that each truth will be taken as an opportunity to move through something. Truth always opens us to our vulnerabilities. For example, when the person in the couple who is afraid to look in the other's eyes finally has the courage to say, "I'm afraid to make love with you because I can't find your soul in your eyes," a door is suddenly opened. It could be slammed shut, of course. Or it might open even wider if the person who hears that truth has the courage to speak the truth in return. "That's because I'm afraid of falling in love with you, because if I fall in love with you, I might lose you, and that would be unbearable." A moment of intimacy, of depth, is created in a relationship precisely because a moment of truth has been shared.

The truth is an ever-widening spiral that releases us to our vulnerabilities in one another's presence. Each time we tell a truth we become more transparent, more visible, more at the mercy of one another's love. Whether it's a simple embarrassing truth: "I'm embarrassed about going to the pool with you because I'm scared I don't look good in my bathing suit"; or a larger, more vulnerable revelation: "Princess Diana's death terrified me because I've always been afraid that I would die at thirty-six"—we open the secret packets of our selves to one another. We ask that these secret, fragile selves, too, can be loved.

Truth is a journey toward magnificence. We move from truth to truth as stepping-stones in a rushing creek that will carry us from one bank to another, from the place where our personalities are content to the place where our souls can soar. That's why, contrary to many current fantasies about what sustains romance, in the future world of relationships honesty will not only be the best policy—it will be the *only* policy. Our fantasizing days are over. As the soul teases us to higher levels of self-awareness, we are also being invited to share more and more truth with one another. This conscious exchange of truth is, in fact, how we move more and more to the soul level.

What this means in practice is that we will entertain not only the obvious truths about another person—he's handsome, he's generous, he's a good lover—but also the truths that we are continually uncovering together. "Oh, I see. It's painful for you to talk about marriage because of your mother's six divorces. I'm sorry."

Instead of reacting, we will explore. Instead of judging, we will be curious. Bringing this degree of honesty into the midst of a relationship means taking the risk, moment by moment, event by event, of expressing yourself fully in any given situation. The risk may be simple—asking for a response: "I've just given you a lot of advice and I need you to tell me how it's affecting you. I feel a little out on a limb." Or it may be more scary, talking about the *kind* of relationship you want to have, for example, when you can sense that your partner doesn't share your feelings: "I'm enjoying getting to know you, but I'm not ready for us to be lovers. I've created a lot of problems for myself in the past by getting sexually involved too soon, so I need what we're doing here to be called a friendship. No matter what you're dreaming up or hankering after, I need us just to be friends."

It may not feel good to say all these things. You're taking an emotional risk. What if this person doesn't understand or can't give you what you want? How will you feel if he says he heard your advice, but might not be able to respond to it for three weeks—or a lifetime? And how will you react to his revelations if they don't coincide with your dreams? It might not feel good to have your erstwhile suitor tell you that because of *his* problems in the past, he just wants to be friends.

Honesty is bravery. At times it can mean taking the risk that your lover will leave if he knows how you really feel. But in all these new relationships, we are being continuously urged toward revealing these truths because each truth is a doorway not only to further transparency with another person but also to a deeper awareness of ourselves. That is, to our soul dimension. As we embrace each new revelation, each new chapter of truth, we have a choice. Instead of closing down, we can open up. Instead of becoming reactive, we can expand. And each time we choose in the direction of expansion, we experience ourselves as being able to love more.

Although honesty must be the hallmark of our new relationships, there's an important distinction that has to be made here. In the past decade or two, being "open and honest" became an emotional fad. In the name of truth, people said anything they felt like at the moment, randomly expressing comments, criticisms, or complaints that often attacked or devastated another person. This resulted in a great deal of emotional violence. But our spirits, our souls, remind us that we also have responsibilities in the emotional world. When it comes to honesty, always speak your truth with an awareness of your beloved's vulnerability. It's not only you who are taking a risk when you speak the truth; the person who listens is vulnerable, too. What's difficult for you to express may also be extremely painful to hear. If you keep this in mind, you will create a state of mutual trust, a protected and continually expanding space in which, over time, more and more truth can be revealed.

Honesty begets honesty. Your own honesty will begin an ever-expanding circle of knowledge and awareness about the person you love. Having seen you take a risk, he or she will take one also. The more you can reveal your own truths, the more your blindness about your partner will dissolve. That is because the more you actually know about your partner, the more your capacity for love increases. The more you can expand to receive another's honesty, the less you will resist expressing your own. And the more you reveal about who you truly are, the more vivid and satisfying your relationship will become.

Generosity

Generosity is abundance of spirit. It is giving with no ulterior motive, expecting nothing in return. We often think that generosity is a consequence, that because life or a certain person has been generous with us, we can now be generous in return. Since our own cup is filled to overflowing we can give of the excess. Finally, because we have so much, we figure that giving won't hurt. But true generosity is just plain giving all the time, as if we were a fountain, a river, an ocean, as if there were no end to what we have to give, as if we had nothing to consider but giving itself.

In the old paradigms of relationships, where giving was governed by the personality and we were often directed by emptiness and need, there was an unconscious tit-for-tat agenda. I didn't get my needs met, so I can't—or won't—be generous with you. In our new relationships, where the soul is in charge, we can be generous because we know that there are no insatiable needs and there is nothing to protect. Since we remember that we are really all part of one great soul, we can see our beloved as ourselves, and know that we can give without end, without harm. And we know we can give everything. We can give not only our material possessions but our words, our bodies, our insights, our time, our money, our empathy, our listening, and our compassion.

My own parents, married forty-seven years, always called one another "Dearie." "Dearie," one of them would call out. "What is it, Dearie?" the other would always respond, as if to say, Whatever you need, I will give it to you, whatever you ask I will do it gladly. The antiphony of their "Dearies" was a sweet music that punctuated my young life. To me it meant that they saw one another as equal in spirit, and that in that great love they were always willing to serve one another. They called each other "Dearie" to their dying day.

Generosity is a circle that returns unto itself. The more we give, the more we have. And in this state of generosity, willing spiritual sharing, we ourselves are healed. For when we are generous, we can see the vast abundance that is also there for us. This is true generosity because no one is excluded. We are all drawn together, united by it. Through it we have a taste of union. It grants us ease and gives us the grace of knowing that life is more than an endless struggle. Indeed it is gracious, generous, and kind.

Empathy

Empathy is feeling with, embracing another's hardship as your own. As the hunter, moved by the fear in the wild deer's eyes, lets him run free in the forest, when we have empathy we can abandon the endless frustrating project of getting our own needs met and gradually develop our capacity to see another's suffering. We do this because we recognize, for a moment, an hour, or a lifetime, that others also have needs. We pull ourselves consciously out of our relentless self-focus and decide to attend to—to feel with—them.

Suddenly we are willing to see and to serve. Instead of being perpetually dragged around by an endless, insatiable, silent yearning that never gets fulfilled, we know the grace of being able to look at another's suffering and say, "I see your hurt. I see the tragic battering of your spirit. I understand your need and I'm here to feel it with you, to show you that you are no longer alone."

This is the bath of empathic compassion that arises from the level of our own soul and washes over the ailing personality, wiping its tears, washing its feet, cleansing its wounds. With such an elegant embracing of another, we can truly feel with them.

We do this on the spiritual level. In a moment of grace, we open the frame of the context and start asking the larger questions: How can I love in this situation? What must I understand about this other person in order to gather him into a healing embrace of emotion? How can I quietly, gracefully join with him in his suffering?

Forgiveness

Forgiveness is an expansion of the heart. In relationship, it is the giving of grace, of understanding, of a second chance—or fifty more chances—to anyone who has hurt you.

In any relationship longer than three weeks old, there's a need for forgiveness. That's because we all hurt one another, whether we intend to or not. Since we are all emotionally wounded we all have emotional trigger points that can be unwittingly activated by anyone at any time. Since you grew up in poverty it may be painful for you when your lover decides to drive your new car without asking. You may explode. He may not know what the big deal is, and only if you can see his side, too—he was excited and so proud of you for saving the money to buy it—can you forgive. Or, at a more painful level, it may feel unbearable—and totally unforgiv-able—that your wife decides to have an affair instead of dis-cussing her discontents with you. Only when you look at the way that, for years, you refused to listen to her will you per-haps be able to open your heart to forgiveness.

Forgiveness requires opening—and communication. You can *want* to forgive, but you can't actually do it and feel it all the way down to your heart unless you know what the real issues are. This is conscious forgiveness.

Forgiveness is like a soft-focus photograph. In the soft state of forgiveness, our own pain is muted because we are able to translate it into a larger context. Instead of staying focused on our own needs and hurts, where many actions do indeed seem unforgivable, we open the frame of our reference to include the other person's situation. What was my lover dealing with when he couldn't give me enough attention? What happened in my wife's past that made her unable to listen, even when I needed her to so badly?

Forgiveness expands us so we can see the other side. You may feel righteous right now, being on the receiving end of the pain, feeling the hurt that was dealt you. But at some other time, you could just as easily be on the other side, playing the role of the person who needs to be forgiven. In fact, it is often the case, as we move ever more onto the soul level, that we will have one side of the experience in one relationship and its exact opposite in our very next relationship. So it may be that this time you were betrayed, but next time you will be the betrayer, or that this time you were the abandoner, but next time you will be abandoned.

The personality keeps tabs, adding up deficits and failures, wanting recompense. But the soul is aware of everything that went wrong on all levels of experience. Instead of judging, it invites us to look at the situation from the awareness that we are all imperfect; that sooner or later we will all make most of the human mistakes. Forgiveness *is* that awareness, nurtured in your own consciousness, reached for at the right moment, delivered as a gift to your beloved.

In the annals of forgiveness, here is a stunning tale: A woman married her college sweetheart, and they were happy for a time. They had two sons, and from the minute the children were born, the woman got overly involved with them. Feeling cut off, the man begged his wife for attention and more sex, but when, after half a dozen years, none of the above were forthcoming, he regretfully divorced her. A few years after her divorce, she was pursued by and subsequently had a long relationship with a woman who was a lesbian. Although she was surprised by her own involvement, the formerly married woman recognized that this new relationship filled a deep need. It nurtured parts of her that had been terribly abused and ignored by her mother, who had been an unconscious, hysterical alcoholic.

She had had a great feminine incompletion, which her female lover had filled. The more she healed, the more fully she understood that her wounds with her mother were the source of her inability to bring her own warmth into her relationship with her husband. As she gradually went through her healing process, she began to realize that she was not, in fact, a lesbian. In full appreciation of what they had given to each other, the two women poignantly ended their relationship, and she felt great regret for her withholding treatment of her former husband.

She wrote him a letter asking for his forgiveness. At first, he expressed rage and then disgust at his wife's sexual involvement with a woman. She stayed open and listened. "I moved through all the states of the male ego," he says, "and then realized that it was just that—male ego. The important thing was that I still loved her." As she continued to reveal herself to him and talked about how her other relationship represented a healing of the very wound by which he had been victimized in their marriage, his increased clarity allowed him to see her with compassion. "In fact," he said, "it was as if all I could see was this woman, my wife, who had never been mothered. My response moved from self-righteousness to forgiveness."

They married again. "Of course it's not perfect," he says. "At times, when things are still difficult, I can get back into my male ego, but the truth is that we both have grown from this experience. We never take one another or our bond for granted. Even our sexual relationship has changed. There's a new softness. Because my wife finally got what she needed, she can now give to me. We've passed through the eye of the needle. We're having this relationship at a whole new level. I can't say we're 'in love' anymore in the romantic sense. But the love we have now is so strong, it can carry us anywhere. Through my forgiving the one thing that, as a man, I thought I could never forgive, we have come to a love that's so strong, it can carry us anywhere."

Thanksgiving

Thanksgiving isn't a day; it's a lifetime. It's not a holiday; it's a way of life. It is the state of waking every morning and knowing that there is only one response to life and that is . . . to give thanks. We are here as a gift. We need to receive the gift. To give continual thanks for it. And to return it.

One of the things that gave me profound irritation on a recent particular day was the fact that each time I thanked someone for some kind, albeit very ordinary thing they did—the fact that they put the fish on ice, so it would be cool all the way home, the fact that they washed my windshield beautifully, instead of in a half-baked fashion, the fact that they hurried with my lunch when I said I was in a hurry—every single person's response was "no problem." It's as if we're living in a world that is a problem; life is a problem; we are a problem to one another, and there are only two categories of experience: a problem and not a problem.

Life is not a problem. It is a miracle, a gift, a teaching, a celebration. Thanksgiving acknowledges the miracle of life—every gift—and saying "you're welcome" is a kind of thanksgiving in itself. It acknowledges the gift of thanks. It says that we live in a world of beautifully interacting thankfulness. It affirms that we live in a world awash with treasures, with miracles and blessings, that we are blessed with an endless array of people, moments, experiences, surprises, magic, curiosities, and beautiful coincidences to which our only, delighted, ecstatic, and unchanging response should be thanksgiving.

The personality keeps tabs, counts beans, worries that there isn't enough, thinks that life is a problem, believes that this moment or that transaction is. The soul knows that everything in life—including life itself—is a stunning privilege, something for which we must always give thanks.

Thanksgiving is the soul's acknowledgment that all is well, that life is a grand and beautiful gift, that all we have to do is carry ourselves to the altar of life with a shouted breath of thanksgiving. Give thanks.

Consecration

Offering your relationship to a higher level of service is its consecration. A spiritual life implies the recognition that we are all a piece of the cloth. Our brother's suffering is ours. We are moved not just by the narrow needs of our own personalities but by the expansive awareness that in some sense everyone's anguish is our own. When we consecrate a relationship to this higher level of service, we honor the sacredness of our union.

Years ago, when I was in training as a psychotherapist, a very famous psychoanalyst confessed to me that one of the reasons he loved being a therapist was that every time he went to his office to treat his clients' depression, his own depression lifted. When he saw how difficult each of the lives of his patients was, he suddenly saw his own life in a new perspective. When he saw how courageous they were in the face of their own difficulties, he was inspired. When he received their thanks for what he had done for them, his own heart was opened to thanksgiving. The healing he gave was the miracle of healing that he received.

So it is with all of us. Our own sufferings are only a part of that vast kettle of suffering that is the human condition. There is always someone whose situation is more excruciating than your own, always a soul who needs your caring, always an offering of service that can transform your own life.

The young women who work in Mother Teresa's order all have their hair cut off in a ceremony of commitment to their work. You want to weep when you see all their beautiful locks fall to the floor. But they all say they have been freed. They have been freed from "bad hair" days into the service of love. They have been freed from the niggling, tedious self-focus that is our life's work when we are directed by the personality, into the grandeur of a life's work that is a service to humanity. They have been freed to love.

I once sat next to a man on an airplane who mentioned casually that he'd been married eighteen years and was terribly excited about returning home to his wife in California. He'd been working on the East Coast for several weeks and was coming home for the weekend, only to return back East on Monday morning.

"That's quite a trip to make just for the weekend, isn't it?" I said.

"Yes," he responded, "but I can't wait to see my wife. I'm looking forward to having a wonderful weekend with her."

"That's lovely," I said, "and quite unusual."

He nodded. "We're fortunate," he said. "We're as much in

love as we've ever been, and the reason is that we have a secret."

When I asked him what it was, expecting any number of wild possibilities, he answered with a single word: service. "We both have work that is larger than we are. I direct a national program for children of poverty and she works in development programs in Third World countries."

He said they once counted up that they'd been apart for twelve of their eighteen years. But they'd both acknowledged that what they were pursuing in their individual lives was so enriching personally that when they came together there was always passion and excitement. They trusted each other with their extensive absences because they were each so committed to the level of the other's service that on every level their own reunitings were always very powerful. Unwittingly but consistently, this man and his wife were living their love in a way that made certain it would always have mystery. Their commitment to service ensured that it would always be radiant, new, and electrically charged, not only with the luminous sheen of romance but with the enduring power of a commitment that has been willingly surrendered to service.

Great love is service. It is serving with the recognition that, really, there is nothing else worth doing in our lives. Aligning with our souls always liberates us to service—and to the magnificent kinds of service that can only explode our hearts with joy.

Joy

Joy is the true pure state of our souls. When we are in joy we understand that there is nothing to understand, that everything's perfect just as it is—and that it always will be. We can relax and en*joy* ourselves—that is, bathe ourselves in the feeling that all is well with the world.

Since human life does have some real limitations, we can't live in joy every moment, but we can aspire to joy by acknowledging it whenever it occurs. We can also create more moments of joy—exquisite interactions that bring us to the state of joy—and we can make the movement to joy a conscious living priority instead of a happy accident.

We can strip our lives of whatever stands in the way of our receiving joy—too many things, too much noise, too many cardboard obligations, worry, no sense of humor, not enough quiet time with our own precious bodies and souls. With the words we say, with the way we conduct our passion, by opening ourselves to the blessings of nature, by looking into each other's eyes—we can create more joy.

Joy is the true condition of our souls. It is what we will return to. It is what we can taste of now. A couple I know certainly did.

They fell in love in college and went back and forth a hundred times about whether or not to get married, because they had fallen in love so young. They'd both missed a typical dating adolescence and felt scared to make a commitment to each other. They broke up a number of times, each trying other lovers, but always got back together again. When the man was in his early thirties, he was in a terrible car accident which rendered him a paraplegic. For more than a month, he trembled in a coma, and it was unclear whether or not he would survive. The woman, who at the time was in one of her "I'm not with him" phases, came to his side and stayed there for months as he fluttered in and out of consciousness. During this time, she felt a powerful new love for him. "It was beyond words," she says. "Very pure." When he finally regained full consciousness, he was moved across the country to be cared for by his parents, several thousand miles away.

The woman accompanied him on the journey, and after spending a brief time there with him, helping get him settled into a routine of assistance and physical therapy, returned to the West Coast and tried to pursue another relationship. She got a job, was successful, but never seemed to click with any of her suitors. Meanwhile, unbeknownst to all her colleagues and friends, she continued to have a relationship with this man. She wrote to him frequently and even now, years later, she still flies across the country once a month to be with him. In his apartment he has a photograph of her and speaks of her as the love of his life. "In spirit I'm married to her," he says. Both of these people are in the odd situation of appearing to be single and yet being married on a soul level. "We'll never live together," he says, "I've faced the fact that my life has limits." The woman also acknowledges that no matter how much they have both tried to move on from this relationship, there is something ineffable about it. They are each other's true love.

Usually when we think of making the vow or taking a stand of "in sickness or in health," we think of it as being attached to marriage or at least to a daily shared life. This couple never made such a vow. They never married. Instead, as the various painful and beautiful layers of their relationship unfolded, they discovered that theirs was the deepest and most enduring love in each of their lives.

Whether steadfastness in this very difficult situation is the completion on a soul level of another story from another time, is irrelevant. What is both relevant and stunning is the beauty of the love that keeps bringing this woman back to this man. "It is *always* a joy," she says. And it's not that she isn't open to engage in other relationships. In fact, they both recognize that from time to time she may do this. But for each of them, theirs will always be the relationship of the greatest depth.

Doubt Is the Condition of the Process

In the realm of our relationships, we can never know with absolute certainty whether we've chosen the right relationship or made the right choices for ourselves. Mysteries abound; this is the soul's power and whimsy. But whatever we choose, moment by moment, the more we are in possession of these ten luminous attributes, the more we will move through each moment with grace and be enlarged by it. When we live by these attributes, we can't do it wrong—we are always following our soul's path.

Conversely, as we move through each spiritual rite of passage in a relationship, one or more of these attributes is further developed. Through practice, each one of them is enlarged. So it is that the woman who lacks joy, faced with the bankruptcy of her spouse, may come to discover joy in the simplest things, and therein develop the capacity for joy. Or the man who refused to become self-aware, through the shattering end of a relationship, may be vaulted into self-awareness. Or the person who never gave thanks, through the terrible illness of her spouse, may be moved to a thankful heart.

Each time we pass through one of these portals of transformation in a relationship, our spiritual capacities expand. As they do, we become magnificent human lovers, divinely inspired.

Chapter 9

Transformational Challenges

Living the Questions of
Illumined Relationships

Movement to a higher level of consciousness in any arena requires a period of initiation. An initiation, often called the dark night of the soul, is an extremely upsetting time, during which we are challenged in any number of areas, often simultaneously. The process is unbelievably intense, we often feel crazy, wonder what we're doing, doubt the rightness of our actions, and wonder if we'll ever make it to the next level.

Actually moving into all these new and extraordinary relationships is such a process of initiation, and at times we *will* feel crazy, lost, overwhelmed, and angry. That's because we're not just revising the etiquette of a particular relationship, we're revamping our relationship lives as a whole. As we go through these upheaving changes, we not only have to ride them out, we also have to endure the difficult feelings they arouse.

That's why, even as we're moving into a dazzling future, we're still poignantly nostalgic for the past. That's why we're still looking for "family values" at the same time we're looking for spiritual consciousness—somehow we know that they are both to be found in our relationships. That's why even though this may be your fourth marriage, you may still want to wear white and promise "until death do us part."

As we go through this initiation period, there are several highly charged areas that consistently appear as points of challenge. They are like barometers, showing us where the trouble spots are or where they are likely to occur. Like red flags along the racetrack, they show up to signal potential danger, to tell us to beware. They are the obstacles, nightmares, potential horror stories which, if we have the courage to face and resolve them, will deliver us, in joy, to our new relationship lives.

Sexuality

First, sex. What will be the role of sex in the relationships of the future? Will it continue to be the main characteristic that defines a relationship as it always has in the past? Or will our relationships run wild across sexual boundaries in such a way as to make our sexual behavior meaningless? Since we're in the habit of using sex as the line of demarcation between what constitutes and what does not constitute an intimate relationship (We're having sex; we must be "in a relationship." We're not having sex, so we must not be), the role of sex in our new unions will be of even greater importance.

Sexuality is a spiritual energy; it is the power to create life. On a simple, biological level we recognize it as the force for the reproduction and survival of the species; and this is the historical reason why we have always used it to delineate the existence of a relationship. But now that we know the species will survive—in fact there are far too many of us—we can also experience sex as pure physical pleasure, as emotional bonding, and for some highly developed souls, as the path to spiritual transcendence.

Sex provides romantic attraction on the personality level, but the soul also uses this energy, which is so powerful and godlike, to draw us toward and align us with a particular person when we have soul and personality work to do. That is because our life's work and the lessons before us are so difficult, demanding, and challenging that if it weren't for the magnetic attraction of sexual energy, we might never undertake any relationships at all.

Once we're in a relationship, however, sex isn't just a force of attraction. It becomes a vocabulary within the relationship. We can choose to experience it as lust, control, and a battle for power, or we can see it as love, surrender, or even a swim in the field of unified consciousness. However we choose to enact it, it can always be a gateway to a deeper dimension of self. We can feel more, open more, connect more, and as we join, lose control and surrender, our personalities dissolve for a moment and we can capture a taste of soul union. In the sexual encounter, as nowhere else, we glimpse that we are not alone.

Because of its historical meaning, romantic power, and spiritual possibilities, sex is a landmark experience for any relationship. But because we are consciously creating our new relationships, our sexuality brings up the question of what we have always called "fidelity." In the past, we defined fidelity as a promise to cleave sexually to one person and no others. But now, if we're not going to define relationships specifically and only in terms of a sexual bond, what will fidelity mean?

Indeed, as we open the boundaries of what we allow to occur in our relationships, new configurations of emotional intimacy will also create new meanings for our sexual commitments. We can have many lovers in a lifetime or even several at once. The significant difference is that instead of having sexual fidelity as the identifying mark of a relationship, a given as it was in the past, in the relationships of the future we will be free to choose what we want sex to mean.

For many people, fidelity will continue to mean what it always has meant—the choice to be sexual with only one partner. But for others, it will mean emotional faithfulness, fidelity to some other agreed-upon commitment, to raising your children, for example, while you and your spouse or partner each have an outside lover. Or it may mean sharing your sexual energy with several partners at the same time. It may even mean celibacy, a personal commitment not to engage in sex with anyone for a brief time—or a lifetime.

I know one highly spiritually developed couple who have had a joyful, committed, and nonsexual marriage for twelve years. They see their union as being the grounding for their sacred service, counseling in an AIDS hospice. Although they were sexual with one another in the past, they felt their sexuality was a spiritual distraction, and they have consciously chosen to move their relationship to this new level.

Whatever your individual choices, the new meaning of fidelity is to be faithful—to yourself, to what you believe, to whatever commitments you and the person you love have consciously decided to make. This new frontier won't be arrived at easily. It will require honesty—and realism. It will ask us to reveal more of ourselves than we have in the past, to take greater chances of truth and vulnerability.

Understandably, there's a natural fear that with the loss of standard sexual monogamy we'll all become sexually irresponsible. But we've already been sexually irresponsible; we just haven't admitted that we were. In reality, quite the opposite is true. As our new relationships lift us to a new level of spiritual awareness, they will actually invite us to new levels of consciousness—and responsibility—about our sexuality. As we venture into new territory, we will be able to learn more and more about what sexual energy *really* is, including its healthy boundaries and ecstatic possibilities. As a result, we will make clear, conscious, personal decisions about how to use it. "This is a sexual friendship," we might say, or "This is a marriage where the bond of sexual monogamy absolutely defines it," or "This is a nonsexual friendship," or "This is an emotional marriage—I love you, but I don't choose to be sexual with you," or "I have a number of lovers; would you like to be one of them?"

Whatever we say, however we choose to live out our sexuality in relationship, we will do it with far more consciousness than ever before. It won't just be the impulse that launches us into some halfhearted union or the crowbar that pries us out of it. It will be what it is: powerful, exquisite, grand, a life force that has the power to create not only a new life apart from us but new life—transformation—within us.

If we can find the courage to move with honesty and realism in creating our sexual relationships, then we will be protected as we have never been before. We won't have to get lost, derailed, or inappropriately detained by our sexuality. And we can invite sex—or sexual abstinence—to bring us to a new depth of experience. The relationships that are the future of love will grant us the opportunity to recognize sexuality as the exquisite power it is, to treasure it, to bless it—and to use it in full consciousness. As we do, the other arenas we share will also emerge in their full beauty. We will be able to see the emotional, companionate, and friendship realms as worlds of preciousness and value in their own right, neither clouded nor falsely illumined by our sexual preoccupations.

The bottom line is that when we function at the soul level, we are being challenged to look beneath the ineffable attraction, the "chemistry," that causes us to fall in love, and discover the true spiritual agenda of our sexuality. For our sexuality—when the soul runs the show—is always, impeccably taking us where we most need to go.

Relaxing of Boundaries

In these new forms of relationships, instead of living out the myth of exclusivity, we will be living out the reality of expansiveness. We will acknowledge that along the path of development, our souls are encouraging us to make multiple connections and commitments to a number of people. This, in some sense, has always been true. The old tradition of a "night out with the boys" and a "night out with the girls" was always a sort of passing acknowledgment that we need more than one overworked be-all and end-all exclusive person.

This truth will now be enacted much more openly; people will still come together in primary relationships, but they will also allow for a greater number of people to participate in both partners' lives in a variety of ways. Ex-stepchildren, former lovers, friends of a friend, two lovers of the same person—all these are relationships we might easily be asked to embrace; they all embody love in its myriad mutating forms.

Instead of seeing these alternative forms as dangerous to the primary relationship, we'll allow our core relationships to open up and include these other people, trusting that we can have more love with a greater number of people, and also more kinds of love—whether it be a sexual connection, emotional intimacy, the nurturing of friendship, or a fraternal or sisterly bond. As we do, we'll open our hearts just a little bit wider in a lot of new ways, trusting that this will take us somewhere good.

As relationships move away from exclusivity toward community and oneness, we move toward a greater awareness of who we are as human beings, that we are souls living in a human community. Rather than separating ourselves from everyone, we're now moving in the direction of joining with everyone.

This kind of oneness can be frightening. We've always been

told that we need to have boundaries in our relationships, and that sanity lies in protecting those boundaries. In fact, the protection of boundaries has been a psychological principle for decades, and the thought of relaxing them can feel quite threatening.

The notion of boundaries is correlated with the need for emotional healing. In all the ways we were hurt or violated, weren't blessed or affirmed as children, we feel a great need to hold our own ground. We don't want to get hurt, invaded, trampled on, or ignored, ever again. We therefore put up fences and draw lines in order to create boundaries—actual and emotional. These boundaries can be about our bodies, as in "You can't slip your hand under my sweater without asking." Or about money, as in "You can't take a dollar out of my billfold without letting me know." Or "Don't run up the credit cards unless we've agreed about it." The boundaries can be about territory: "This is my side of the closet, of the bed, of the bathroom sink." Or about emotions: "Don't ever tease me, don't call me silly or stupid, don't say admiring things about other men in my presence, or you'll make me feel worthless the way my father always did." Or "Don't flirt with other women when I'm with you because you'll make me feel invisible, the way I always did with my sisters."

Basically, we create boundaries to try to bring ourselves to the level of emotional well-being that makes us feel able to love and worthy of being loved. Boundaries serve us well in this context. Within the defined, protected area, we can grow and stand up for ourselves. By so doing, we can gradually increase our stature, and in time we won't feel so vulnerable or have to create such rigid boundaries.

Unfortunately, we often get stranded at the boundary stage of creating, protecting, and defending ourselves, not realizing that there are far grander possibilities that lie beyond the boundaries: the sense of union that comes when many are gathered together, the exalted feeling when we share our joy with several people at once, the love ignited by two people who already love one another, when, in a simultaneous moment, they recognize their love for a third.

The notion of defending and protecting boundaries has been highly touted in our culture, particularly in situations of abuse and co-dependence, where the defending of boundaries is appropriate. But as a general principle of intimacy or of soulful relationships, the notion of boundaries is rigid—an abstract, intellectual construct which keeps us in combat mode. Boundaries draw lines. They don't bring us to the altar of kinship. They keep us at arm's length from love.

A far greater inner spirit is now telling us that we need to relax, trust, and keep on tiptoeing across the boundaries, even though each little step may be frightening. One of the reasons we're scared is that we're afraid that relaxing our boundaries means that we're not looking after ourselves. This idea in itself is hard to let go of. And so each of us will have to rely on self-awareness, honesty, and realism to guide us in discerning what is truly appropriate for us in any given situation.

The forms of our relationships will change; they will dissolve and mutate; and as they do, they will offer us new avenues of contact, more opportunities to love. They will expand; they will be able to contain more love. And as they move us toward greater contact with greater numbers of people, our relationships will be encompassing, welcoming, gracious, and warm, a great castle with a hearth and a feast laid out on the table. Sitting down to the feast, being able to meet the grandeur of such love without shying away in the fear of losing our boundaries will be one of our greatest challenges. But as we surrender, we will fall into the arms of great love.

Reluctance to Let Go of Old Forms

Because of our emotional expectations of relationships, we are committed to their form. Form is the container. It is the pattern or structure which embraces, defines, or supports whatever the form may contain. A refrigerator carton is the form in which a refrigerator is stored and transported. A Kleenex box is the container in which the Kleenex is stored and served up.

There's always an interesting connection between form and content and sometimes the form *implies* the content. We expect an eggshell to contain an egg, for example—a yolk and a white. But sometimes the relationship between form and content isn't so clear. A birthday party package all wrapped up in bows can contain almost anything. So can a plastic bottle or a tin can. More interestingly, when I was a young girl, in spring we always planted a packet of seeds called "The Surprise Packet." Although this envelope of seeds was exactly the same size as all of the others, its contents were always various and unpredictable. It wasn't morning glories or marigolds. It was a whole raft of unexpected and beautiful flowers.

Unlike my magical packet of seeds, in traditional marriage, form is foremost. In fact, it is the form of marriage which, for most of us, defines any relationship as having more than passing significance. We define a good relationship as the one that endures over time. Not because there is love in it necessarily, or joy or truth or consciousness. But because its visible structure, the house of its being (or its carcass), has survived.

Just as we would, for example, expect a symphony hall, precisely because of its form, to have great acoustics, or the Houston Astrodome, because of its form, to be weatherproof, we expect marriage, just because of its form, to be a good thing and to "make us happy." We believe that a relationship's possibilities have to do with its form—marriage—and not with its content—two suffering, growing souls who must continually try to learn how to love one another.

Going past form is terrifying because it is through form above all that we have always known our relationships: we're married; we live together; he is my husband, my boyfriend, my spouse. To leave form behind means that we will have to operate from new levels of responsibility and self-awareness, being aware enough to choose, being ongoingly conscious enough to evaluate, being honest enough to keep re-creating the form of a given relationship, or of our whole relationship lives as the needs of our spirits revise. We don't particularly want to do this; it's a lot of work. One of the gifts of our past relationship forms is that they made life easy; we could just relax into them.

Formlessness requires us to move with the grace of a dancer, of a milkweed pod, of the wind, touching people and relationships in ways that are unusual—and perhaps only momentary. This is exceedingly unfamiliar. But much of the beauty provided by such encounters, such unconventional moments, or even lifetimes has eluded us through our straitened commitment to form. If we want the incredible experiences that stepping out of the conventional forms has to offer, we must also be willing, conscientiously, to develop the attributes—honesty above all—that will allow us to enjoy these experiences as the true spiritual gifts that they are.

Conscious Parting

Another challenging part of our initiation is that because we may have many love relationships, we may also have many partings. The American Indians have a saying that happiness is being able to live beside a river that flows both ways. As it applies to our relationships, this means that we could find happiness if we could both enter into and depart from our relationships with thanksgiving and joy. Indeed, what an incredible leap in our evolution it would be if we could both fall in love and break up in love—with tears of thanks, with generosity.

Recently, I was speaking to a young man of thirty-two who had spent seven years living with a woman eight years his senior. During that time, he had been a father to her two children and given her step-by-step encouragement in developing a new career. When her career finally brought her the kind of success she'd always dreamed of, she dumped him in one fell swoop on Valentine's Day.

"The thing that's so painful," he said, "is that we didn't do it with sweetness, with a ceremony, with love. I understand the seven-year itch, I see that she's forty now and she wants to be free, but it seems to me that for all the beautiful times we had, we could have made it more beautiful at the end."

When we have loved deeply, it's only natural that we go through great anguish in parting. That's because on the personality level we feel so strongly, we hope for so much. We become so dearly attached. It is also because our personalities are romantic, sentimental, nostalgic, and deeply touched. We just "can't get over" all of the wonderful things: the sound of her voice, her red hair, the way he sang in the shower, the way he made love to you, or smiled, or always said your name in a certain beautiful way. We get attached to certain aspects of another person, the things that are unique, that we think we'll never find again in anyone else, the things we especially liked and enjoyed. And so, as a consequence, when it's time to leave, instead of letting go, we try to hang on. We wish we could just toss out all the parts we don't like and keep on enjoying the ones that we do, but, unfortunately, that isn't an option.

The soul doesn't give us this option because it keeps moving us ever onward to the people and experiences that will take us on the next steps of our journey of evolution. And so at some point we have to face the fact that we have to keep or let go of it *all*—of the entire relationship and of the whole, wonderful person, of all the parts that delighted us as well as the ones that drove us around the bend. That's why even when we see clearly that a relationship is far too difficult and tormented to continue, or even when we know that we have completed what we were meant to do together—that it really is time to move on—it can still be extremely painful to finally say farewell.

Because endings are always so painful, they bring us to a crisis: we can break up with anger, rage, and blame (like a personality), or we can leave consciously in love (like a soul), remembering that this other soul, too, lives on and that real love never dies.

Such conscious parting is much more difficult than the muddled way we often ended our relationships in the past, because the soul asks us to leave in love, to consciously say goodbye, to lovingly say thank you. It can be even more complicated by the fact that since our souls are always remembering the oneness that is really our true condition, it sometimes seems insane that we have to stop loving anybody or, more accurately, to give up the specific form in which we have loved them. As a result, these farewells can be even more excruciating when there is a deep soul connection, and when there is, it often takes even more time to unravel all the heartstrings that have attached us to one another.

In such situations, it's almost as if our souls are saying, "But I love him so much, why should we have to be separated in this life? I don't want to have to wait to see him again until we're souls in the ether again. My soul misses him already; we're supposed to stay connected." Because our souls remember union, when we see that we have to leave we sometimes agonize on an even more exquisite level; and at times the process of release can seem interminable.

"I've been ending this relationship for longer than I've been in it," one woman said to me recently. She was speaking of a twelve-year relationship that began when she was still married and had an intensely passionate and beautiful affair which precipitated the end of her marriage. When she finally divorced her husband, her lover was devastated by the fact that, rather than choosing him, she went on a journey of personal growth which included her having several other relationships. Having been so totally in love with her that he had left his wife in the hopes that she would marry him, her lover went on to marry someone else, creating a short-lived, frustrating union which ended in his second divorce.

Years later, when the two of them were finally both unmarried, they came together once again. The woman felt sad and guilty about the way their previous relationship had ended. When she saw that the sexual passion was still alive, she took up with her ex-lover once again, hoping to establish a new relationship and heal the pain of their past. As they gradually worked through their bushels of hurt feelings, the question arose as to whether or not they would now make an attempt to become a conventional "couple." But no matter how hard they tried, they found that all their original differences—he smoked and drank and she was a vegetarian health food fanatic—made it impossible for them to have anything that resembled a marriage.

After several years of painful fights and farewells, the man finally said to her one night, "I guess it's my soul that can't bear to say goodbye." They wept for hours in one another's arms, and after this cleansing were at last able to let go. Because they had finally acknowledged their soul connection, they knew that they would always hold a deep love for one another in their hearts. Despite their separation, they knew that their souls would always be bonded through the love they had once shared.

The truth is that wherever love has once existed, it remains. Love is eternal. It doesn't go away. When a relationship ends it just isn't around in the same form it once was, tucked into the same shoe box it was in when you were in "a relationship." Even at the end, our souls know that any coming together with another soul has been a gift of spirit, a taste of the togetherness which is the soul's true condition.

Ending with Grace

What if you could look at your whole life of relationships as a grand hotel that you keep coming back to just because you like to spend time there? Each time you go back, you try a different beautiful room for a different amount of time, knowing that there are always more rooms, that you can share them with different people, and that each time you will be gifted with different, wonderful experiences. Imagine how peaceful you would feel if you could fully accept the reality that we will *all* have a number of relationships—and probably several kinds of them—over a lifetime. What if we didn't have to be in agony just because one of our relationships didn't give us everything or because it came to an end? What if we knew that the endings weren't failures, but beautiful steps along the path? What if we could be grateful in the beginning, in the middle, *and* at the end? What if we didn't have to hate one another just because a relationship did end? What if we could quietly, graciously comprehend that we spent exactly the amount of time we were supposed to spend—and now it's time to move on?

With every ending, we are invited to choose between force and grace, between consciousness and stupidity, between fear and love. Graciousness and ease are possible, but in order for us to actually accomplish our partings with grace and ease, we must conduct them from the soul level. To the degree we can remember that, for each of us, love is the longing to return to our one grand soul, we can make all our partings more loving, more conscious, and more gracious.

There are four essential steps to this process:

1. *Accepting That the End Is Necessary*

This is the acknowledgment phase. Here you consciously announce to yourself that the relationship is over. You recognize that you've given each other all you were meant to give. It's time to part ways. You speak this truth to one another, acknowledging that your journey together is now complete. The lessons were indelible and true and even the harshness was part of the great beauty of love.

2. *Taking the Necessary Steps to Make the Ending Happen*

In conscious parting, you make the appropriate decisions and take steps together to effect the relationship's completion. You may decide not to speak to one another for six months, or you may stay in contact all along the way. Either way, you negotiate this *together*. Because you both know the ending is painful, you consciously keep to your agreement, knowing that by doing so, you will assist in your healing.

3. Claiming the Gifts of the Relationship

Whether you choose to do this in a ceremony together or in private, by yourself, you part in thanksgiving. You openly, consciously, and wholeheartedly acknowledge each life-changing moment and well of grief that shaped you during the relationship, and you bless all of it. Who have you become as a result of this relationship? What is the nature of your transformation? How did the other person effect it? What is the abiding awareness of this person that you will always have with you?

4. Allowing It to Rest in Completion

You allow yourselves to grieve over the separation, remembering that love is eternal. You are patient, letting the process define itself. You are willing, knowing each step of the parting has something to teach you. You are trusting, knowing that someday you will love again.

Conscious parting allows you to end a relationship without a sense that you failed. It will allow you to stay present through the ending, to move through it as it moves through you. Instead of feeling victimized by the ending, you can move forward with a sense of beautiful completion, aware of the gifts as much as the loss, more excited by the future than mired in the past. These conscious completions will also allow you to stop hanging on to the tattered relics of every old relationship and dragging them with you into the next one. And when you finish the process and allow the form of your present relationship to dissolve, you will see the birth of some new relationship emerging—a mentor, a business partner, spiritual guide, or sacred friend. Or, for any number of reasons, you may decide that it's most appropriate to go your separate ways permanently. Perhaps your lessons came through wounds that were, in fact, so deep that you need lasting distance, or perhaps it's important now that you take the gifts of this relationship and firmly move forward with them on your own. Either way, you will do it in peace, and with no lasting bitterness.

A number of years ago, it was my privilege to have a relationship with a man much younger than myself. He stepped into my life at a time of great difficulty when the overwhelming demands of a burgeoning career and deep grief over the death of a longtime friend converged to leave me exhausted and vulnerable to several episodes of ill health. He entered first as a friend. We shared some ordinary pleasures and found comfort in one another's company. Later we became lovers, in spite of our mutual awareness that this was a relationship most likely without a future since both of our paths were clearly marked out and running in quite opposite directions. Nevertheless, we shared many wonderful times, delighting in one another's company. For each of us a difficult past season was being relieved by the playfulness we shared, and as our romantic epoch unfolded, we were pleased to discover that we were both reviving and that this relationship had bridged us from a season of stress to a place of such well-being, confidence, and pleasure that—we shyly admitted—we both felt ready to fall in love again.

At this point, my brave suitor had the courage to talk about the fact that having finally recovered from his last relationship, he was now ready to go exploring in the world of relationships and possibly find his life mate. Minutes before he mentioned this, I had been feeling exactly the same thing. We had prepared one another for a relationship of some deeper magnitude. So, on a lovely spring day, we sat down and told this truth to one another. We talked about what a pleasure our relationship had been, how renewed we felt as a result of having been loved by each other and how the time of our being together had passed. As he put it: "We've climbed to the top of the mountain that we were supposed to climb together and now we have nowhere else to go."

So it was that with tears, compassion, passion, and generosity, we said goodbye. It was a clean, conscious, and beautiful cut that has allowed for the subsequent emergence of a beautiful lifelong friendship. But the vase in which our own love once blossomed has always remained as a sacred vessel, reminding us of the beauty we shared, no matter what lives we each have moved on to.

To be able to receive a relationship with exactly what it has to offer you, to know that you have received it, to say thank you in love, and, in love, to recognize its completion, is one of the grandest, albeit most poignant, ceremonies of love. Among the many gifts that this relationship brought me, the greatest was that it was lived in a perfect circle from beginning to end, with love as its doorway and love its portal to departure.

Every relationship, minute or gigantic, awful or wondrous, has a profound bounty of gifts to offer. Each relationship is preparing you for something. It may be molding you for the moment when you can finally make a commitment to marriage. It may be urging you to make a profound commitment to yourself. Or it may allow you to come to peace with the fact that you have had a whole lifetime of unusual relationships.

Wherever your relationship is taking you, whatever direction it beckons you to follow, whatever the mark it leaves upon you, it has a meaning and magnitude of its own. So it is that rather than seeing any of your relationships as a mistake that you drifted into blindly and perhaps later will have to slip out of, you can create the emotional attitude that enables you to see each one of them as a gift. This will allow you to give thanks for the arrival of your beloved for an afternoon, three weeks, an unforgettable summer, or a few years—just long enough to be the father or mother of your children—or for an entire lifetime.

The Opinions of Others

Another challenge will be dealing with the opinions and judgments of others, particularly family, about your choice of relationships. How your parents feel about who you choose to love has always been a matter of great significance. In the past, an ideal mate was someone your parents would be happy to see at their Thanksgiving table, and those who couldn't make the parental cut often faced a startling ending to their relationships. A displeased father could whisk his daughter off on an extended European vacation, hoping her attentions would be diverted by something or someone else, or threaten a son with disinheritance.

But these days there are other ways inventive parents can

find to undermine the relationships they don't like. Becoming the "mother-in-law from hell" is one; withholding financial support at some critical juncture—when it's time for a wedding, to help with buying a house, or to continue to help with college in spite of your choosing the wrong fiancé—is another. But now, as if dealing with difficult parents isn't enough, we also have the opinions of our children to deal with. As we take them with us into our new relationships, they can be yet another prickling source of disapproval.

As relationship pioneers, we can be doubly under assault, continually challenged by a painful two-generational attack, sandwiched between conventional, prejudiced parents and critical, unhappy children. The truth is that so few of us have completed the demanding work of making peace with our parents that by the time we're creating our own relationships, we're rarely detached enough to cope with such intense levels of parental disapproval. And it's easy to feel upset, if not flat-out devastated, by this lack of deeply longed-for support.

As a consequence, all the remarkable new relationships we're creating are insisting that we have courage, that we become so strong and committed that we can withstand disapproval, that we can champion our decisions—even when they're tested to the hilt, challenged most excruciatingly by those we have always loved—our parents and children.

Knowing that this is true, if you're not sure that you really want a particular relationship, you'd better think twice. You may have to go to bat and even become emotionally bloodied because of the partner you've chosen. You will have to be able to hold your own against criticism, judgment, rudeness, and all manner of emotional manipulation by people who are afraid because your particular relationship might rock their emotional boats.

This is especially true if your parents have never worked out their feelings of disappointment or regret about their own relationships. Some of us have parents whose consciousness is so undeveloped that their most courageous act is to follow the status quo without wavering. If that's true in your case, there's no doubt your parents will have a problem with your newfangled relationship. And they probably won't try to hide it. Their own fears will be the measure of how strongly they try to resist you. Just as we're afraid of change, of creating all these new and unusual forms of relationship, the people—your parents—who preceded you down a far more conventional relationship path will be even more afraid.

A lovely young woman I know went home with her fiancé to meet his parents. His mother had scheduled a haircut and manicure for her, and suggested that she choose some clothes from *her* closet so the young woman would look right when her future mother-in-law took her to lunch to meet a few friends.

With her hair sprayed into a helmet, this woman passed the most uncomfortable lunch of her life. Later that day, when she complained to her fiancé, he said she was "too sensitive." They had a terrible fight and almost broke up, and it wasn't until they got back home again three days later that they realized they were still in love.

So make no mistake: one way or another your extraordinary relationship will, sooner or later, come under attack. You can't just slip it in under the family front door unnoticed, because most likely it will represent the very departure from tradition your family members have always feared most, and when people are scared, they attack.

While it's reasonable to hope that, as opposed to your parents and children, your dear friends and peers will be in support of your new, unique relationship, this, too, won't necessarily be the case. You will be under their scrutiny. And some of your friends, not just because they're conventional, but because they're sad or afraid about losing you in the way that they've always known you, will express it by taking umbrage at your unconventional partner or the unfamiliar format of your new relationship. Even—and maybe especially—your closest friend may feel displaced, uncomfortable, or angry. While we've always had such reactions to our relationships in the past, the fact that many of our new relationships are assuming such unusual forms makes us all the more sensitive. We're not always sure just how to defend them.

So, as you roll with all the criticism, wade through all the prejudice, and work through all the feelings with your friends, it will be helpful to remember that it is nothing less than a relationship revolution that we're having here. We're all on the front lines. What this boils down to is that we will all have to be prepared to present our relationships with consciousness, awareness, and commitment. Most of all, we will have to be prepared for the inner doubts such outside assaults can arouse. Here is where your own self-awareness—the beautiful inner consciousness that has allowed you to know each step of the way that what you are building is wonderful and right, as true and correct for you as any relationship can be—must hold forth. Here is where your honesty must come forward. This is where your forgiveness—of those who can't or won't understand—must arise. Here is where your courage, thanksgiving, and joy must prevail.

The wonderful thing is that it is precisely through surviving such painful emotional battles that you will be doing your part in the transformation of all our relationships as a whole. You will be opening the path, widening and deepening the chalice in which, all together, we hold our lifetimes of love. Your perseverance and everyone else's—all gathered up—will bring us together. And in this gathering, in this quiet, steady, and beautiful movement, we will all gradually see that all the exceptions are the new rules. We will come to be at ease with the new forms of love. We will see—and we will actually experience—that love, indeed, is formless.

Shyly, beautifully, with a calm and sacred magnificence, with our judgments laid down, with our hearts stretched open a little bit wider, we will begin to embrace everyone. This will be the awakening of our unified spiritual consciousness. It will be the exaltation of our love.

Chapter 10

The Greatest Love

Soul love is the greatest love there is. When we build a relationship with full awareness of our souls, we have a profound sense of connectedness which transcends the limits of all our human, romantic relationships and gives us a glimpse of our true spiritual magnificence. At the level of the soul, we all recognize one another and know that each relationship, little or grand, is but a tiny snowflake in the vast avalanche of ebullient white light that is all the love in the world.

Each day, as our relationships change and we change with them, we are proving that conscious love is possible, regardless of its form, regardless of its surprising and curious contents. We are discovering that there is a particular time and an exquisite uniqueness to each individual pairing, that an ending can also be a beginning, that each time the energies shift and we create a new relationship, we are aligning with new life, new possibilities. The process may be agonizing, but even the agony can be a gift. It is a reminder of the depth of our emotions, of our capacity for passion and forgiveness, for generosity and expansiveness, and of our longing to love and to be loved.

Although we can't fully see ourselves yet or recognize where we're going, we are all a part of the history of humanity in the making. We have been called upon to pioneer an epoch of human experience in which the forms are falling apart so that our souls may ascend to the next level. In this process of consecrating and releasing the old, worn-out forms of relationship, we shed tears of loss and then catch hold of the tail of a kite that is carrying us ever upwards to the further reaches of consciousness. Privileged to be involved in this process, we rise to the possibility of knowing true love in our lives.

The love that brings us together, whatever it looks like, is nothing less than soul energy. It has traveled for lifetimes in order to find expression in this particular moment, in this particular relationship. Grand and generous, it pours out over every difficulty and challenge, dissolving pain, creating beauty, transforming everything it touches along the way. No challenge is too great for true love, no distance too far to cross.

As souls, we know a secret: our human experience is a teaching in which we discover and remember that we are spiritual beings. Because this is true—because, indeed, this is the one truth that encompasses all others—we can stop torturing ourselves as we live out all these new, extraordinary relationships, knowing that our souls have arranged them. Each and every one of them has been designed to show us our depths and to bring us to our knees in recognition of the fact that we are spiritual beings living human lives.

The beauty in all this is that *through our relationships* we are arriving at the spiritual level. As our personalities are healed and the painful layers all fall away, we are beginning to understand that the spiritual part of each of us will never be fully satisfied by any one human relationship. We see that each relationship is a step along the journey to that satisfaction and so we can stop beating ourselves up each time a relationship ends. As each of us moves through our own particular dance card of relationships, we will gradually discover that the breaking down of traditional forms is a unique opportunity to get acquainted with a larger truth—that we are all, in some way, in relationship with one another. We will bask in that truth. We will consciously move toward it. Indeed, this is the work of these latter years of the twentieth century; and the dawning of the new millennium will reveal love to us as never before.

Our souls know who we are. The more we rise to our own soul-driven magnificence, the more the mystery of life emerges in the form of a presence that is somehow far more powerful than the sum of all our relationships put together. As we surrender to the essence of this mysterious force, we feel melted, joined, united. We feel generous and whole, we become our true selves, strangers to no one, in love with Love, in touch with the incontrovertible truth that, indeed, we are all One.

A mighty power is calling us, not back to the way we used to be, but forward into the light of our souls. Our individual relationships are serving as the beautiful human templates for this calling, gently guiding us toward the community of spiritual beings which, all together, we are becoming. The sum total of all our failed expectations and bitter disappointments, our ragged endings and broken hearts is, in fact, our arrival at the doorstep of true love.

And to ensure that we will arrive there, the soul has arranged that the future of our relationships will be a forced march, a Viennese waltz, a *Peyton Place* soap opera episode, and a monastic retreat all rolled into one. And this will be our return to love. For our souls are asking for nothing less than the absolute meltdown of our individual consciousnesses into the sea of the One Great Soul. And when finally we arrive, we will look back and see that we were always on our way there; we were always becoming something beautiful. The love that called our souls to uncompromising truth, forgiveness, surrender, and compassion is the same stunning force in which we will now experience our peace.

We will arrive because we have expanded. And we are already expanding. We are already becoming living, walking examples of that divine expansiveness. Even as everything is breaking down, we are opening, letting in what was once outside, embracing the unfamiliar, forgiving the unforgiven, gathering into our embrace all who were once excluded and shut out, receiving into the folds of our hearts the lonely, wandering sheep who were shunned.

As we expand, we melt. Our hearts open. Our thinking changes. Our obsessions subside, our addictions quietly pass away. This is the slow, elegant, loving process through which, little by little, we let go of the old and welcome the new. We open our hearts and allow in a few more people, just a few more relationship experiences, just a few more kinds of relationships. We learn that there are no mistakes, and our hearts become a circle so large that there are no more boundaries, no differences, no judgments. We know the graciousness of that great undivided familiarity, in which there are no more strangers, only friends.

We stretch, and to our amazement we don't break. Instead, we grow. Suddenly, everything becomes easier, and our hearts, which once we believed could love only one person, or were battered so badly we thought they could never love again, expand so fully that the whole world is welcome. In such a state of openness, we see that we have only forgotten how to be together, we faintly and beautifully remember that once we *were* all together. We remember the way we were in a universe of incredible softness where there were no edges, no walls, no mind games, no rules. In that incredible world, we were happy. We loved one another. It wasn't a feeling. It was a state of being called joy.

The future of love is this all-encompassing embrace. For when we have expanded so much, we will finally arrive at a place where the heart can open its doors to everything and everyone. Our souls have been taking us on this journey and Love is the magnificent destination to which they have been leading us. Now we can feel joy. Now, at last, we can be satisfied. Now, finally, we are home.

A Prayer for Union

God of light Who calls us into being,
    Who guards us on our way,
We pray for peace in our hearts in this season
    Of the transformation of our relationships,
    Of upheaval, of crumbling, of falling away.
As our relationships pass like sand through our fingers,
May we be blessed with the grace to know,
    That this falling apart is, in truth,
    Our journey of coming together,
    Of finally returning home.
May we be startled awake by the memory of love,

The One Great Love that called us into being,
And is our only real destination.

May we have the strength to give up our search for
    "the one,"
Because, all together, we are The One,
   And You are the True Beloved,
   The ever-awaiting One,
Who allows us to move from love to love,
Knowing that You, our true selves,
Will always be there to meet us.

May we be released from the agony
   Of wanting, hoping, dreaming, expecting.
May we instead be brought into the present moment
   Of acceptance, grace, and simplicity,
Knowing that the sweet breath of love we breathe
In each relationship
Is the breath of the One Great Love.

Allow us to see that love is eternal,
Show us again and again
   That love is larger than all its forms.
And may we go through these seasons of change,
   In a state of surrender, of joy,
   With the exact and perfect trust
That every step is ordained for a beautiful reason.

God of light Who calls us into being,
We pray for joy, for wisdom and compassion

In the relationships that we do have.
We pray for the willingness to grow,
    For we want to be grander than we already are.
We pray for the sacred water of the One,
    For our baptism, for our cleansing,
    And our healing,
    For our melting, for our joining.
We pray for light, for both inner and outer
        illumination,
    For the brilliance to see, to know, and to feel,
    To imagine and to remember
That You are with us each step of the way,
That we are not alone.

We pray for appreciation, acceptance, and forgiveness
Of all the steps, and missteps, and sidesteps
    That we have taken on the long journey
That will bring us to our sweet reunion,
    That will finally carry us back home.